The TOUR OF WALES *Recipe Book*

The TOUR OF WALES Recipe Book

Compiled and edited by
Glyneth and Alan Torjussen

Gomer Press

Published in 1980 by
Gomer Press
Llandysul
Dyfed

Printed in Wales by
J. D. Lewis & Sons Ltd.
Gomer Press
Llandysul
Dyfed

First impression May 1980

ISBN 0 85088 972 3

The editors would like to thank Yr Ystafell Gymraeg for help in the
production of the cover photograph. Photography by David Williams,
Craely's Studios, Cardiff. Illustrations by Lynne Sieger.

Whilst every effort has been made to ensure accuracy neither the editors
nor the publishers can be held responsible for errors, inaccuracies
or omissions.

Not all of the recipes included are available at all times at the
respective restaurants.

Introduction

Have you ever eaten a superb meal at a restaurant and wished you could persuade the chef to give you the recipe? If the answer is yes, then this book is for you.

We have travelled around Wales and invited the chefs at many of the best hotels and restaurants to give us their favourite recipes.

Wales has an amazing selection of very good places to eat. The tremendous variety of food offered at these restaurants is reflected in the selection of recipes in this book. We include recipes from France, Italy, Germany, Greece, Spain, Malta, Latin America, Indonesia, China and many variations on traditional Welsh and English dishes. We have something for everyone—from lobster in shrimp and wine sauce to vegetable soups made for a few pence.

The Tour of Wales Recipe Book is intended for every housewife who likes cooking, although we suspect that a few chefs may also buy a copy.

Finally, we should like to thank the chefs and restauranteurs who have helped and encouraged us so much in the preparation of this book.

Glyneth and Alan Torjussen

The Tour of Wales
from Chepstow to Mold

The Cedars Hotel, Chepstow, Gwent
16 Poussin stuffed with peach served with peach brandy and cream sauce
Cripple Creek Inn, Raglan, Gwent
17 Fillet of beef Wellington
Beaufort Arms Hotel, Raglan, Gwent
18 Gambas al ajillo
Walnut Tree Inn, Llandewi Skirrid, Gwent
19 Haddock smokies
20 Quails impatachio
Three Cocks Hotel, near Brecon, Powys
21 Roast guinea fowl—Normandie
Hotel Metropole, Llandrindod Wells, Powys
22 Crown of Welsh lamb in green pepper sauce
23 Sautéed lamb kidneys with cream and mustard sauce
23 Chilled apple and raspberry tart
The Blue Bell Inn, Llangurig, near Llanidloes, Powys
24 Salad dressing
Royal Oak Hotel, Welshpool, Powys
25 Chicken marengo
Lake Vyrnwy Hotel, Llanwddyn, Powys
26 Smoked trout pâté
Hand Hotel, Llangollen, Clwyd
27 Fillet of brill Prince of Wales
The Owain Glyndwr Hotel, Corwen, Clwyd
28 Game broth
29 Avocado Edeyrnion
30 Dee salmon, Glyndwr
31 Duckling Merioneth
Ruthin Castle, Ruthin, Clwyd
32 Roast shoulder of Welsh mutton
The Plough Inn, Llandegla, near Wrexham, Clwyd
34 Boeuf à la Bourguignonne
35 Orange chiffon pie
Wrexham Crest Hotel, Wrexham, Clwyd
36 Pork chop Villa Borgese
Golden Grove Inn, Rosset, near Wrexham, Clwyd
37 Golden chicken estragon
The Liver Inn, Rhydtalog, Mold, Clwyd
38 Steak and kidney pie

from Deeside to Anglesey

The Chequers, Northophall Village, Delyn, Clwyd
39 Sauté of chicken in cider with baked apples
41 Egg and honey pudding
Bryn Morfydd Hotel, near Denbigh, Clwyd
42 Indonesian Satay
Hotel 70 Degrees, Penmaenhead, Colwyn Bay, Clwyd
44 Chicken Supreme Opera
45 Beignets soufflé
Empire Hotel, Llandudno, Gwynedd
46 Marinated gammon steaks with glazed pineapple and watercress
47 Wings of skate with capers and blackbutter
Alfredo Restaurant, Conwy, Gwynedd
48 Osso bucco
49 Mont Blanc
Plas Maenan Hotel, Maenan, Llanrwst, Gwynedd
50 Saint Tudno sauce—for pork
50 Anglesey eggs
Waterloo Motor Hotel, Betws-y-Coed, Gwynedd
52 Coq au vin
53 Kidneys Turbigo
Eagles Hotel, Penmachno, near Betws-y-Coed, Gwynedd
54 Lentil soup
54 Steak in wine
Castle Hotel, Bangor, Gwynedd
55 Bara brith
Le Patron Restaurant, Wern Y Wylan, Beaumaris, Anglesey
56 Gigot d'agneau à la maison
57 Les pêches farcies
Henllys Hall Hotel, Beaumaris, Anglesey
58 Welsh rarebit
59 Baked ham and parsley sauce
Bulkeley Arms, Beaumaris, Anglesey
60 Rösti
The Lobster Pot, Church Bay, near Holyhead, Anglesey
61 Lobster Winterthur
Glantraeth, Trefdraeth, Bodorgan, Anglesey
62 Menai Pride mussel pâté
63 Spare ribs in honey and cinnamon
63 Peach Snowdonia Range

from Snowdon to Dolgellau

Royal Victoria Hotel, Llanberis, Gwynedd
64 Snowdon Pudding
The Stables Restaurant, Llanwnda, Caernarfon, Gwynedd
65 Stables strawberry gâteau
Linksway Hotel, Morfa Nefyn, near Pwllheli, Gwynedd
66 Fresh orange with rum flavoured syrup
The Dive Inn, Tudweiliog, near Pwllheli, Gwynedd
67 Aljotta—fish soup from Malta
Porth Tocyn Hotel, Abersoch, Gwynedd
68 Captain's relish
68 Norwegian style beetroot
69 Roast loin of veal with lemon sauce
70 Damson and apple mousse
Bronheulog Hotel, Abersoch, Gwynedd
71 Medallions of fillet of beef Campania
Hotel Bryn Derwen, Llanbedrog, Gwynedd
72 Pear and walnut salad
73 Rabbit stew with claret
74 Banana trifle
Villa Pandana, Garndolbenmaen, near Portmadoc, Gwynedd
75 Italian trifle
Moelwyn Restaurant, Criccieth, Gwynedd
76 Kipper pâté
The Royal Goat Hotel, Beddgelert, Gwynedd
77 Gelert's pineapple
The Saracen's Head Hotel, Beddgelert, Gwynedd
78 Chicken Royale
Sygun Fawr Country House Hotel, Beddgelert, Gwynedd
79 Dressed crab
79 Syllabub
The Hotel Portmeirion, Penrhyndeudraeth, Gwynedd
80 Aubergines fourées
81 Terrine de Sibier
82 Canneloni alla Vescovo
83 Bœuf des Marinieres
Bontddu Hall Hotel, Dolgellau, Gwynedd
84 Smoked haddock chowder
85 Fried cheese stuffed mushrooms with devilled sauce
86 Grilled Mawddach salmon en brochette with saffron rice
and lemon butter sauce
87 Pork fillet à la maison

from Dinas Mawddwy to St David's

The Red Lion Hotel, Dinas Mawddwy, Powys
88 Traditional Welsh cawl
Trefeddian Hotel, Aberdovey, Gwynedd
89 Ice cream soufflé Grand Marnier
Ynyshir Hall, Eglwysfach, near Machynlleth, Powys
90 Tomato Gervais
91 Venison in pastry
Conrah Country House Hotel, Chancery, Aberystwyth, Dyfed
92 Casserole of veal
The Lamb Hotel, Llangeler, near Llandysul, Dyfed
93 Chicken Maryland
Emlyn Arms Hotel, Newcastle Emlyn, Dyfed
94 Whole grilled Teifi sewin with lemon and almond stuffing
   and cold cucumber sauce
95 Austrian coffee cake
The Cliff Hotel, Gwbert-on-sea, near Cardigan, Dyfed
96 French onion soup
97 Sewin and cucumber sauce
Ferry Restaurant, St Dogmael's, Dyfed
98 Mushrooms in garlic sauce
Ye Old Salutation Inn, Velindre, Crymych, Dyfed
99 Salutation lobster
Fishguard Bay Hotel, Fishguard, Goodwick, Dyfed
100 Salmon steak Lady Jane
101 Braised lettuce with cucumber sauce
Plas Glyn-y-Mel, Lower Fishguard, Dyfed
102 Grapefruit cocktail
103 Green beans Chinese style
Whitesands Bay Hotel, Whitesands, St David's, Dyfed
104 Escalopes sauté oriental with egg fried rice
106 Black Forest gâteau
Cartref Restaurant, St David's, Dyfed
107 Carrot and tomato soup
108 Beef casseroled in cider with apples and parsley
109 Fresh pineapple and peaches in rum
Warpool Court Hotel, St David's, Dyfed
110 Chicken Gujarat
111 Cheese-cake with Kirsch

from St David's to Swansea

St Non's Hotel, St David's, Dyfed
112 Scallops maison
113 Ham and asparagus soufflé
114 Pheasant poivrade
115 Fraises Marquise
Cuffern Hotel, Roch, near Haverfordwest, Dyfed
116 Chateaubriand with chasseur sauce
Druidstone Hotel, Druidston Haven, Dyfed
118 Scallops à la crème
119 Fresh strawberry and melon flan
**Chez Gilbert Restaurant, Pembroke House Hotel,
    Haverfordwest, Dyfed**
120 Rabbit peasants style
Coach House Inn, Pembroke, Dyfed
121 Chilli con carne
The Royal Gate House Hotel, Tenby, Dyfed
122 Sole fourée
Buckingham Hotel, Tenby, Dyfed
123 Noisettes of lamb Dinbych
Malin House, Saundersfoot, Dyfed
124 Scampi Provencale
125 Lemon mousse
Robeston House, Robeston Wathen, near Narberth, Dyfed
126 Pork with apricot and almonds
127 Orange gâteau
Ivy Bush Royal Hotel, Carmarthen Dyfed
128 Leek and potato mutton broth
129 Surprise eggs
130 Risotto casimir
131 Braised Welsh calves livers with marinated raisin sauce
Plas Glansevin Hotel, Llangadog, Dyfed
132 Melon salad with hot herb bread
133 Apple pudding
134 Bread and butter pudding with pears
135 Pancakes in orange sauce
The Cawdor Arms Hotel, Llandeilo, Dyfed
136 Norwegian prawns
Stradey Park Hotel, Llanelli, Dyfed
137 Les escalopes de veau Marlborough
**Heatherslade Bay Hotel, Southgate, Swansea,
    West Glamorgan**
138 Chocolate crumb cake
139 Plum compote with rich almond cake

from Swansea to Cardiff

Osborne Hotel, Langland Bay, Swansea, West Glamorgan
140   Roast duck Osborne
Dragon Hotel, Swansea, West Glamorgan
141   Ris d'agneau Prince de Galles
Drangway Restaurant, Swansea, West Glamorgan
142   Turbot with mussel sauce
143   Welsh chicken
Hotel Executive, Aberavon, Port Talbot, West Glamorgan
144   Fillet steak Cleopatra
Seabank Hotel, Porthcawl, Mid Glamorgan
145   Suprême of chicken Porthcawl
Quaintways Restaurant, Llantwit Major, South Glamorgan
146   Pork tenderloin with prunes
147   Jamaican baked bananas
The City Inn, City, near Cowbridge, South Glamorgan
148   Marrow Provençale
The Bear Hotel, Cowbridge, South Glamorgan
149   Braised ox-tail
Caso Paco Restaurant, Barry, South Glamorgan
150   Stuffed peppers
151   Tomato sauce
Four Lanterns Restaurant, Barry, South Glamorgan
152   Afelia with Cyprus style fried potatoes
153   Dolmades
Sully House Restaurant, Swanbridge, South Glamorgan
154   Crêpes aux fruits de mer
155   Carré d'agneau en croûte
Caprice Restaurant, Penarth, South Glamorgan
156   Tagliatelle Alfredo
156   Vittello Pizziaola
157   Zabaglione Caprice
Glendale Hotel, Penarth, South Glamorgan
158   Stracciatella soup
Plymouth Arms, St Fagans, South Glamorgan
159   Tŷ potatoes
159   Welsh apple tart
Harvesters, Cardiff
160   Kedgeree
161   Jugged hare

from Cardiff to Tintern

Gibson's Restaurant, Cardiff
162 Artichoke soup
163 Maggie Gibson's chicken pie
164 Brandy tulips
Savastano's Ristorante Italiano, Cardiff
165 Spaghetti alla Carbonara
165 Flambé à la maître d'hôtel
La Locanda Restaurant, Cardiff
166 Fillet mignons à la Beaufremont
Positano Ristorante Italiano, Cardiff
167 Saltimbocca alla Romana
The Spot Restaurant, Cardiff
168 Fillets of sole casimir
169 Médaillons de veau Gourmet
Royal Hotel, Cardiff
170 Paprika schnitzel
Angel Hotel, Cardiff
171 Cold avocado soup
171 Duck à l'orange
Roman Embassy Italian Restaurant, Cardiff
172 Fillet steak Roman Embassy
Costa Brava Restaurant, Cardiff
173 Entrecôte Apollo
Yr Ystafell Gymraeg, Cardiff
174 Chicken Snowdonia
175 Cutlets of veal Prince of Wales
Lanterns Restaurant, Cardiff
176 Prawn alagratin
Post House Hotel, Cardiff
177 Chicken Cardigan
Six Bells Inn, Peterstone Wentlooge, South Glamorgan
178 Avocado with sea food
179 Fillet de bœuf sauté strogonoff
180 Melon dessert
Conca d'Oro Restaurant, Newport, Gwent
181 Pâté Conca d'Oro
Westgate Hotel, Newport, Gwent
182 Pineapple Mexican
Three Blackbirds, Llantarnam, Gwent
183 Petti di pollo alla Doney
Beaufort Arms Hotel, Monmouth, Gwent
184 Nelson's casserole
185 Tournedos Beaufort
The Old Farmhouse Hotel, Llandogo, near Tintern, Gwent
186 Old Farmhouse chicken liver pâté

A few basic recipes

Stock

Stock is the basis of most soups and many sauces. Brown stock is made with beef bones. Place in a pan and cover with cold water. Add vegetables (onion, carrot, celery), seasoning and herbs if required (bouquet garni, bay leaf.)
Bring to the boil and remove any scum. Simmer gently for at least 3 hours. Strain and keep in a cool place.
Stock can be made with most meats, game, fish and poultry.
Chicken stock is made with chicken bones, giblets, herbs, vegetables and seasoning and only cooked for 40 minutes.

Espagnole sauce

Espagnole sauce is a basic sauce used in the preparation of many sauces.

1 onion
1 carrot
2 oz mushrooms
2 oz butter or dripping
2 oz bacon or ham
2 oz flour
1 pint brown stock
bouquet garni
1 bay leaf
a few peppercorns, salt
¼ pint tomato pulp or tomato puree

Slice the vegetables and bacon. Melt the butter and fry the bacon for a few minutes. Add the vegetables and fry gently until golden. Stir in the flour and continue cooking. Stir in the stock, herbs and spices and simmer for 30 minutes. Add the tomato and simmer for a further 30 minutes. Pour the sauce through a fine sieve. Season to taste.
A little Madeira or sherry may be added if required.

Demi-glace sauce

½ pint Espagnole sauce (or ¼ pint stock)
¼ pint juices from roasting meat

Boil the sauce and meat juices together until reduced by a third.

Béchamel sauce

1 pint milk (or ½ pint milk and ½ pint white stock)
½ onion
½ carrot
½ celery stick
bay leaf, thyme, mace, etc. to taste
salt, peppercorns
2 oz butter
2 oz flour

Heat the milk with the vegetables, herbs and seasoning, bring slowly to simmering point and leave to stand for 15 minutes (to let the milk absorb the flavours.) Strain the milk. In a separate pan, add the flour to the melted butter, cook this roux for a few minutes without browning, then gradually stir into the milk. Heat to boiling point stirring continuously.

Cooking terms used in the recipes

Bain-marie

A shallow pan, half-full of water, kept at near boiling point, in which a dish of food is cooked without using direct heat. This method is often used for cooking sauces containing yolks or creams and also for cooking pâtés.

Bouquet garni

A small bundle or bag of herbs used to add flavour to sauces or stocks. The herbs usually used are parsley stalks, bay leaf and thyme. The bouquet garni is removed from the dish before serving.

Reduction

Boiling a liquid to reduce the quantity by evaporation, a method used to thicken sauces and stocks.

Sauté

To cook quickly in fat or oil over a strong heat, shaking the pan to keep the contents from sticking to the bottom.

The recipes

The recipes in this book have ingredients enough to serve four persons (unless stated otherwise.)

Pâtés and sweets are usually made in larger quantities, often enough to serve eight or ten persons.

Weights and measures

approximate metric equivalents

1 oz = 30 grams
4 oz = 114 grams
8 oz = 225 grams
1 lb = 450 grams
1 gram = 0.035 oz
100 grams = 3 ½ oz
500 grams − 1 lb 1 ½ oz
1 kilogram = 2 lb 3 oz

3 teaspoons = 1 tablespoon = 1 fluid oz
¼ pint = 5 fluid oz = 0.14 litres = 1 gill
½ pint = 10 fluid oz = 0.28 litres = 1 cup
1 pint = 20 fluid oz = 0.56 litres = 2 cups

1 tablespoon = 1 liqueur glass
1 standard bottle of wine = 26 fluid oz = 6 wine glasses

The Cedars Hotel
Chepstow, Gwent

Proprietor Mrs J M Holmes
Manager I I Klava

Poussin stuffed with peach served with peach brandy and cream sauce

4 x 12 oz poussins (young spring chickens)
2 large peaches
½ pint natural meat juices from roasting
¼ pint double cream
2 fl oz peach brandy
2 fl oz vinegar
12 cubes sugar

Poach the peaches and reserve the cooking liquor. Cut the peaches in half and use to stuff the poussins. Truss the poussins and cook in a moderately hot oven, (Gas Mark 5, 375°F) for about 40 minutes.

Make a reduction of the vinegar and sugar until it starts to caramelize. Add the meat juices and bring to the boil. Add the cooking liquor from the peaches, bring to the boil and reduce. Add the cream and bring back to the boil. Add the brandy. Check the consistency and seasoning before serving.

Recommended wine: Bernkastler Reisling

Cripple Creek Inn
Raglan, Gwent

Fillet of beef Wellington

large fillet of beef
butter
salt, pepper
celery, onion, parsley
1 bay leaf
pinch of rosemary
pâté de foie (liver pâté)
puff pastry
1 egg yolk
½ pint veal stock
3 mushrooms, chopped

Trim the fillet of beef, smear generously with butter and sprinkle with salt and pepper. Place in a roasting pan with scraps of celery, onion and parsley, the bay leaf and rosemary. Roast in a very hot oven (Gas Mark 8, 450°F) for about 25 minutes. Remove the fillet from the roasting pan and allow to cool.

When the fillet is cold, spread with a substantial layer of pâté de foie. Roll out the pastry until ⅛ inch thick and wrap around the fillet. Trim the edges of the pastry, moisten with a little cold water and press firmly together. For a shiny crust, brush the surface of the pastry with beaten egg yolk.

Bake on a baking sheet in a very hot oven for about 15 minutes until the crust is well puffed and delicately browned.

To the contents of the roasting pan add the veal stock, 2 oz of pâté de foie and the mushrooms. Simmer this sauce for 15 minutes, strain and serve separately.

Serve with a green or mixed salad.

Beaufort Arms Hotel
Raglan, Gwent

Proprietor Antonio Mas-Perez
Chef Domenico Evangelista

Gambas al ajillo

24 large Mediterranean prawns in their shells
1 clove garlic
fresh parsley
1 glass dry white wine
4 fl oz fish stock
Tabasco
oil for frying

Peel and finely chop the garlic. Finely chop a large sprig of parsley. Fry the garlic and parsley in very hot oil. When the garlic is beginning to brown add the prawns, stirring well to stop the garlic burning. Add the white wine and reduce by half. Add the fish stock and a few drops of Tabasco to taste. Simmer for 3 or 4 minutes.

To serve, place a sprig of fresh parsley in the centre of the dish and surround with the prawns. (Finger bowls should be provided as the prawns are eaten with the fingers).

The same recipe can be used for chicken (Pollo al ajillo). Use 8 fl oz of chicken stock instead of the fish stock and cook the chicken for much longer.

Walnut Tree Inn
Llandewi Skirrid, near Abergavenny, Gwent

Proprietor/Chef Franco Taruschio

Haddock smokies

1 smoked haddock
milk
1 ½ cups chopped and seeded tomatoes
¼ pint double cream
grated Cheddar cheese
salt, pepper

Cook the smoked haddock for 10 minutes in milk. Remove the haddock from the milk and flake the haddock.

Add the chopped and seeded tomatoes and the double cream. Mix well and add salt and pepper.

Place this mixture in four ramekins and cover with grated Cheddar cheese. Bake in a hot oven (Gas Mark 7, 425°F) for 15 minutes.

Walnut Tree Inn

Quails impatachio

8 quails
12 very ripe tomatoes
8 small sprigs of rosemary
16 cloves garlic, unpeeled
1 tablespoon tomato purée
2 glasses white wine
¼ pint stock
salt, pepper
olive oil for frying

Fry the quails in olive oil until golden.

Peel, seed and chop the tomatoes. Add the tomatoes to the quails in the pan and fry for a few minutes. Add the rosemary, unpeeled garlic cloves, tomato purée, white wine, stock and salt and pepper.

Simmer until the quails are cooked, then reduce rapidly until the sauce thickens.

Roast guinea fowl — Normandie

2 fresh guinea fowl
¼ lb fat bacon

for the stuffing:
2 apples
1 onion
bouquet garni
¼ lb mushrooms
salt, pepper

for the Normandie sauce:
pan juices from birds after roasting
¼ lb sliced button mushrooms
2 apples, peeled and sliced
¼ pint home-made Espagnole sauce
3 tablespoons Calvados
½ pint double cream

To make the stuffing, roughly chop the apples, onion and mushrooms. Mix with the seasoning, add the bouquet garni and stuff the birds. (This stuffing adds flavour and keeps the birds moist, but is not intended for eating). Wrap the bacon around the birds and roast in a moderately hot oven (Gas Mark 5, 375°F) for about 1 hour.

To make the Normandie sauce, lightly fry the sliced mushrooms and apples in the pan juices. Add the Espagnole sauce, cream and Calvados. Bring to the boil, pour over the birds and serve.

Hotel Metropole
Llandrindod Wells, Powys

Managing Director D S Baird Murray
Manager Roberto Marchesi
Chef David Bacon

Crown of Welsh Lamb
with green pepper sauce

1 crown of lamb (4 cutlets per person)
½ pint stock
2 glasses dry white wine
1 tablespoon green peppercorns
1 measure brandy
½ pint fresh cream

Roast the lamb in the oven in the usual way. Allow about 20 minutes per pound and 20 minutes over in a moderately hot oven (Gas Mark 5, 375°F).

Remove the meat from the pan and keep warm. Use the roasting juices as the basis of the sauce. Add the stock, wine and peppercorns. Heat and reduce by half. Add the brandy and flame. Add the cream but do not allow to boil.

Serve with a garnish of potatoes and vegetables.

Sautéed lamb kidneys with cream and mustard sauce

for 6 persons:
18 lamb kidneys
½ lb butter
¾ pint cream
2 tablespoons Dijon mustard
oil for frying
salt, pepper

Trim and slice the kidneys, sauté in hot oil to seal and then drain. Melt the butter and cook the kidneys gently. When tender, add the mustard, cream and salt and pepper to taste. Stir gently until the sauce is formed.

Serve on a bed of Patna rice

Chilled apple and raspberry tart

2 lb cooking apples
shortcrust pastry
raspberry jam
1 pint thick custard

Stew the cooking apples and leave to cool. Line a deep flan tin with shortcrust pastry and bake blind. Allow the pastry to cool and spread raspberry jam over the base. Spread the stewed apples on top. Pour the slightly cool thick custard on top of the flan. Place the flan in the refrigerator.

Serve, when chilled, with fresh cream.

The Blue Bell Inn
Llangurig, near Llanidloes, Powys

Salad dressing

3 cloves garlic
¼ pint wine vinegar
1 pint corn oil (best quality)
2 tablespoons castor sugar
1 teaspoon salt
black mill pepper
1 salt-spoon curry powder

Crush the cloves of garlic. Mix the garlic, sugar, salt, curry powder, and pepper to taste with the vinegar. Add the oil.

Store in a large screw-topped bottle. Shake well before using.

Chicken Marengo

Royal Oak Hotel
Welshpool, Powys

Proprietor Mrs S C Price

Chicken Marengo

4 chicken joints
3-4 tablespoons oil
2 sliced carrots
1 chopped celery stick
1 chopped onion
2 oz chopped streaky bacon
3 level tablespoons flour
½ pint chicken stock
15 oz tin tomatoes
2 tablespoons sherry or
 1 glass rosé wine
bouquet garni
¼ lb sliced mushrooms
garlic to taste
salt, pepper
chopped parsley for garnish

Fry the chicken joints in the oil for about 5 minutes, until golden brown. Remove them from the pan and place in a casserole. Fry the carrots, celery, onion and bacon in the oil left in the pan for about 5 minutes, until golden brown. Remove them from the pan. Stir the flour into the remaining fat in the pan and cook for 2-3 minutes. Gradually add the stock, stirring continuously. Bring to the boil and continue to stir until it thickens. Return the cooked vegetables and bacon to the pan and add the tomatoes, sherry, salt and pepper. Pour this sauce over the chicken in the casserole. Add the bouquet garni and sliced mushrooms. Cook in the centre of a moderate oven (Gas Mark 4, 350°F) for ¾—1 hour, until the chicken joints are tender.

Place the chicken joints on a warm serving dish and pour the sauce from the casserole over them. Sprinkle with chopped parsley. Serve on a bed of boiled rice.

Lake Vyrnwy Hotel
Llanwddyn, Powys

Proprietors Mrs J F Moir and Lt Col J C M Baynes
Chef Mrs J F Moir

Smoked trout pâté

2 x 1 lb trout (smoked and carefully boned while hot)
¼ lb butter
2 tablespoons horseradish cream
½ tablespoon salt
¼ teaspoon pepper

Mince the trout finely. Add the horseradish cream, salt and pepper and mix well. Put into pots and cover with melted butter.

Serve with brown toast.

Hand Hotel
Llangollen, Clwyd

Manager David Morris

Fillet of brill Prince of Wales

4 portions of brill
for the sauce:
1 onion, finely chopped
2 oz flour
2 oz button mushrooms, sliced
1 pint fish stock (made with fish bones and skin)
2 medium sized tomatoes, peeled and chopped
1 glass white wine
1 teaspoon chopped parsley
2 egg yolks mixed with a little cream
2 oz butter or margarine

Sweat the onion in the butter but do not allow to colour. Add the flour and cook for a few minutes. Gradually add the fish stock and then add the mushrooms, tomatoes and wine. Simmer for 20-30 minutes.

Boil, grill or braise the fish.

Remove the sauce from the heat and add the parsley and the egg yolks and cream. Serve immediately.

Recommended wine: Chablis 1974

The Owain Glyndwr Hotel
Corwen, Clwyd

Game broth

3 pints stock (game stock if possible)
2 carrots
1 large Spanish onion
2 oz butter
2 oz flour
8 oz diced game
carcase and trimmings of roast game
2 egg yolks
watercress for garnish

Pound the carcase and trimmings.
Fry the pounded carcase and trimmings with the diced onion and carrots
in the butter until brown. Stir in the flour and allow to brown. Add the
stock and bring to the boil.

Skim, then cook for 1 hour.

Strain, add the diced meat and thicken with the egg yolks.

Garnish with a sprig of watercress.

Avocado Edeyrnion

for 6 persons
3 ripe avocado pears
1 green pepper
1 red pepper
½ Spanish onion
¾ pint French dressing
¼ lb button mushrooms
¾ lb shelled prawns
lemon for garnish

Cut the avocado pears in half. Scoop out the flesh, dice and place in a bowl with the sliced onion, peppers and mushrooms. Pour the French dressing over the mixture, season and leave to marinate for one hour.

Mix in the prawns and fill the avocado skins with this mixture. Serve with lemon.

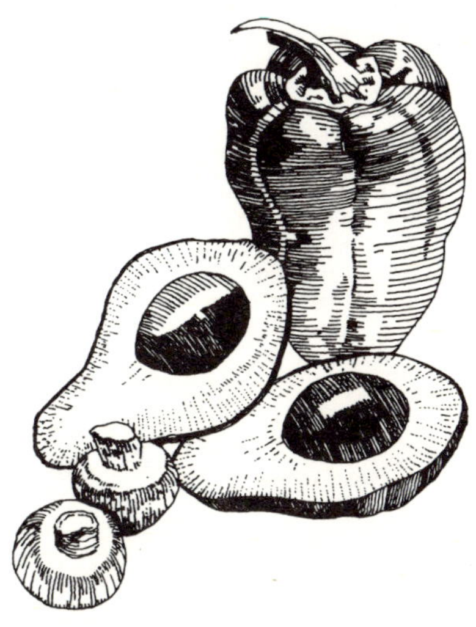

The Owain Glyndwr Hotel

Dee salmon, Glyndwr

2 lb fresh Dee salmon
½ pint vinegar
¾ lb butter
2 shallots
½ lemon
1 teaspoon English mustard
1 bouquet garni
6 anchovy fillets
sprig of parsley
onion
bayleaf
salt
black peppercorns

Cut the salmon into four steaks and poach in vinegar and water with the bouquet garni, bayleaf, onion, salt and black peppercorns.

Mix the butter with the chopped anchovy fillets, shallots, parsley, lemon juice and mustard. Roll this mixture so that it can be sliced. Place the slices on the steaks of salmon.

Serve with new potatoes and salad.

Duckling Merioneth

for 6 persons

1 duckling (weighing about 6 lb)
2 lemons
2 oranges
¼ lb red-currant jelly
4 tablespoons brandy
½ pint demi-glace sauce
1 apple
1 pear
¼ lb cherries
¼ lb pineapple (tinned if not in season)
½ lb black or green grapes
4 oz mixed nuts
salt, pepper

Roast the duckling, removing from the oven when slightly underdone. Allow to cool and remove the breasts. Slice the breasts and lay in a shallow pan. Add the juice of the lemons and oranges and the red-currant jelly. Flambé with the brandy.

Add the demi-glace sauce, the fruit and the nuts. Cook for a further 15 minutes. Season to taste.

Ruthin Castle
Ruthin, Clwyd

Roast shoulder of Welsh mutton

½ shoulder Welsh mutton (about 2 lb)
3 oz lamb kidney
½ large onion
2 oz long grain rice
1 packet parsley and thyme stuffing
1 clove garlic
1 teaspoon garlic salt
2 oz margarine

Bone the shoulder of mutton and remove the skin. Season the whole joint, inside and out with garlic salt.

To make the filling, cut the lamb kidney into ½ inch squares. Sauté the kidney, rice, onion and crushed garlic. Remove from heat and add ¾ of the packet of stuffing and mix in until it coheres.

Stuff the shoulder with the filling and tie firmly. Sprinkle the top of the joint with the remainder of the parsley and thyme stuffing. Cook in a preheated oven, (Gas Mark 5, 375°F) for 50-75 minutes.

Serve with roast gravy.

Suggested vegetables: minted new potatoes, broccoli au beurre, turned baby carrots.

Recommended wine: Gevrey-Chambertin

Bœuf à la Bourguignonne

2 lb lean topside steak (or 2 lb chuck steak)
salt, pepper
1 large onion, sliced
bouquet garni
¼ pint red wine
2 tablespoons olive oil
4 oz salted belly pork
2 tablespoons dripping
8 small white onions
2 tablespoons seasoned flour
½ pint beef stock (or water and beef stock cube)
1 clove garlic
8 oz button mushrooms
1 oz butter or margarine

Cut the steak into 1½ inch pieces and place in a bowl with salt, pepper, the sliced onion, bouquet garni, red wine and olive oil. Cover and marinate for 3-6 hours.

Cut the pork into ¼ inch pieces. Heat the dripping in a heavy based overproof casserole. Add the pork and the small white onions and sauté until golden brown, then remove from the casserole.

Drain the meat from the marinade, toss in seasoned flour and brown in the remaining fat in the casserole. Add the strained marinade and boil for half a minute. Add the stock, bouquet garni and crushed garlic. Cover the casserole and cook in a moderate oven (Gas Mark 4, 350°F) for about 1½ hours. (If chuck steak is used, allow an extra 45 minutes cooking time).

Meanwhile, in a small saucepan, sauté the mushrooms in the butter for about 5 minutes. Return the pork and onions to the casserole and add the mushrooms. Cook for a further 30 minutes. Remove the bouquet garni before serving.

Orange chiffon pie

4 oz rich shortcrust pastry
2 eggs
3 oz castor sugar
strained juice of 1 orange
salt
grated rind of ½ orange
1 teaspoon powdered gelatine dissolved in 1 tablespoon warm water
2 heaped tablespoons whipped cream

Line a flan ring with the pastry and bake blind.

Separate the egg whites from the yolks. Beat the yolks with 2 oz of the sugar, add the orange juice and a pinch of salt. Turn into a double saucepan and cook over gentle heat, whisking continuously until thick. Remove the top part of the saucepan from the hot water. Add the grated orange rind and the gelatine. Continue whisking until light and fluffy and on the point of setting.

Whisk the egg whites with the remaining sugar and fold, with the cream, into the mixture. When it holds its shape, pile into the pastry case. Chill in the refrigerator.

Slightly whipped cream may be poured over the pie immediately before serving.

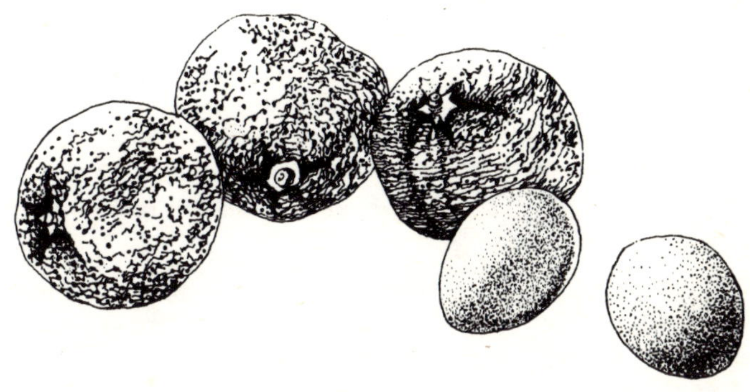

Pork chop Villa Borgese

4 x 8 oz pork chops
2 tomatoes
4 oz boiled ham
4 oz grated cheese
parsley for garnish

for the sauce:
2 egg yolks
2 tablespoons malt vinegar
2 tablespoons water
1 teaspoon lemon juice
salt, pepper
dash of Worcestershire sauce
½ lb melted butter
½ oz chopped parsley
½ oz chopped tarragon

Grill the pork chops until cooked. Place 2 slices of tomato and a 1 oz strip of ham on each chop and place in a warm oven until the sauce has been made.

To make the sauce, whisk the egg yolks, vinegar and water together until smooth. Add the lemon juice, a pinch of salt and pepper and the Worcestershire sauce. Place the bowl containing the mixture in a large dish of warm water, ensuring that the water level is approximately half the depth of the bowl, and continue mixing. Slowly add the melted butter whilst mixing, until a smooth creamy consistency is achieved. Add the chopped parsley and tarragon.

Pour this sauce over the chops, sprinkle with the grated cheese and brown gently under the grill. Garnish with a sprig of parsley.

Golden chicken estragon

4 breasts of chicken
butter
lemon juice
tarragon
egg
breadcrumbs
oil for frying

Split and flatten the breasts of chicken. Cover with a mixture of melted butter, lemon juice and tarragon. Roll the chicken in egg and breadcrumbs.

Deep fry until golden brown.

Serve with a cream and brandy sauce.

The Liver Inn
Rhydtalog, Mold, Clwyd

Steak and kidney pie

1 lb chuck beef
½ lb ox kidney
1 small onion
1 tablespoon brown sauce
1 beef stock cube
1 teaspoon Worcestershire sauce
1 pint water
pastry
salt, pepper

Trim the beef of all fat and gristle. Chop the beef and kidney into ½ inch pieces. Chop the onion.

Place the beef, kidney and onion in a saucepan. Add the sauces, stock cube, water and salt and pepper to taste. Bring to the boil and simmer for 1½ hours.

Turn into a pie dish. Cover with pastry and bake until the pastry is cooked.

The Chequers
Northophall Village, Delyn, Clwyd

Manager John S Hayter

Sauté of chicken in cider with baked apples

1 chicken (3½ — 4 lb)
1 small onion
1 pint rough cider
2 oz butter
4 cooking apples
½ pint cream
salt, pepper
bunch of herbs

for the beurre-manié:
2 oz butter
2 oz flour

Cut the raw chicken into four portions.

Heat the 2 oz of butter in a casserole. Place the chicken portions, diced onion and seasoning in the casserole and seal without colouring. Add the cider and herbs and simmer for 1 hour.

To make the beurre manié, mix the butter and flour to a paste.

Remove the chicken from the cooking liquor. Re-boil the liquor and add the beurre-manié, a little at a time, until the sauce is of a thick coating consistency. Add the cream.

Core the apples and wrap in cooking foil. Bake in a moderately hot oven, (Gas Mark 5, 375°F) for 15-20 minutes.

To serve, place the chicken on a serving dish surrounded by a border of duchesse potatoes and coat with the sauce. When the apples are cooked, remove from the foil and place on the serving dish.

Egg and honey pudding

for the custard:
1 pint milk
5 eggs
2 oz castor sugar
vanilla essence
8 oz honey

for the sweet paste:
½ lb plain flour
4 oz butter
I large egg
2 oz sugar
pinch of salt

for the meringue:
2 egg whites
4 oz castor sugar

To make the custard, mix 2 oz of the honey with the 5 eggs and the 2 oz castor sugar. Boil the milk and add a drop of vanilla essence. Pour the boiling milk on to the egg, honey and sugar mixture. Whisk, then strain.

To make the sweet paste, mix the flour, sugar and salt and rub in the butter until the mixture resembles crumbs. Add the egg and work in as little as possible. Set the paste aside for 30 minutes, then use it to line a small flan ring. Bake blind.

When cooked, remove from the oven and while still hot, smear the bottom of the case with half of the remaining honey (3 oz). Pour the custard into the case and bake in a moderately hot oven (Gas Mark 5, 375°F) for 30 minutes.

Remove from the oven and carefully smear the remaining 3 oz of honey over the top of the custard. Pipe with the meringue.

To make the meringue, whip the eggs and sugar together in a bowl until stiff, (making sure that the bowl is clean and free from grease). It is then ready for piping.

Place the pudding under a hot grill to glaze. Leave to cool and serve cold.

Bryn Morfydd Hotel
Llanrhaeadr, near Denbigh, Clwyd

Indonesian Satay

¾ lb-1 lb fillet of beef or lamb

for the marinade:
2 tablespoons olive oil
1 tablespoon soya sauce
juice of ½ lemon
2 bay leaves
¼ onion, finely chopped
2 cloves garlic, crushed
sprinkling of black pepper
2 teaspoons ground turmeric
½ teaspoon ground coriander
pinch of ground chilli

for the sauce:
6 oz dessicated coconut for preparing coconut milk
½ onion, finely chopped
3 cloves garlic, finely chopped
1 dessertspoon curry powder or curry paste (to taste)
½ pint good stock
2 bay leaves
6 cardamom pods
6 cloves or 3 short pieces cinnamon
1 dessertspoon honey
juice of ½ lemon
¼ lb ground roasted salted peanuts
oil for frying

Cut the meat into pieces 1½ inch square and ½ inch thick. Mix the ingredients for the marinade. Add the meat and leave to marinate overnight or for several hours, turning occasionally.

To make the sauce, first prepare the coconut milk. Place the dessicated coconut in a small container. Add ½ pint boiling water and leave for 10 minutes, stirring occasionally. Empty into a fine sieve and press out the coconut milk.

Fry the onion and garlic in a little oil until clear. Add the curry powder or paste and fry for a few minutes, adding more oil if needed. Add the stock and spices and simmer for 20 minutes. Remove the pods, leaves etc. Add the coconut milk, honey and lemon juice and bring to the boil. Finally add the ground peanuts until the sauce is thick. Cook for another 2 or 3 minutes.

Remove the pieces of meat from the marinade and thread onto skewers, so that the meat lies flat. Lay the skewers on a grill pan. Grill slowly, turning occasionally. Brush liberally with the marinade at intervals whilst grilling.

Serve with salad and plain or savoury rice or with Indonesian rice cubes. To prepare the salad, roughly chop one onion and half a cucumber into cubes. Sprinkle lightly with salt and lemon juice.

Recommended wine: Gevrey-Chambertin

Chicken suprême Opera

4 chicken suprêmes
6 oz finely diced mushrooms
flour
egg
butter for frying
white breadcrumbs

Remove the fillet at the back of each suprême and flatten slightly. Make a small slit in the side of each suprême to form a cavity.

Sauté the mushrooms in butter without colouring. Place the mushrooms in the cavities. Tuck the flattened fillet back on top of the mushrooms. Carefully roll the suprêmes in flour, dip in egg-wash and coat in breadcrumbs. Shallow fry in butter for about 5 minutes on each side and finish cooking in a moderate oven (Gas Mark 4, 350°F) for 10-15 minutes.

Serve with demi-glace sauce made with Madeira or sherry.

Beignets soufflé

for 6 to 8 persons
¾ lb flour
½ lb butter
2 oz sugar
8 eggs
1 pint water
salt
castor sugar
fat for frying

Place the water in a saucepan and bring to the boil. Add the butter, sugar and a pinch of salt. Stir in the flour to give a thick paste. Cook for 1 or 2 minutes. Remove from the heat. Gradually beat in the well beaten eggs.

Drop spoonfulls of the mixture into hot fat. Deep fry until lightly browned. Drain and roll in castor sugar.

Serve with fresh cream and ice cream.

Empire Hotel
Llandudno, Gwynedd

Manager L E Maddocks

Marinated gammon steaks and glazed pineapple with watercress

4 x 4-6 oz gammon steaks
black pepper
1 fresh pineapple, peeled, cored and sliced
  or small tin pineapple rings
Demerara sugar
sprigs of watercress for garnish

for the marinade:

½ pint sweet cider
1 small onion
2 cloves garlic
¼ pint olive oil
2 bay leaves
1 teaspoon French mustard

To prepare the marinade, peel and slice the onion and finely chop the garlic. Add the onion and garlic to the cider and olive oil and mix gently together. Add the bay leaves and mix in the teaspoon of French mustard. Soak the gammon steaks in this marinade for 2-3 hours.

Pre-heat the grill. Remove the steaks from the marinade and season with black pepper. Grill the steaks, turning them over after 5 minutes. Place two rings of pineapple on each steak and dust with Demerara sugar. Grill for a further 5 minutes.

Place the steaks on a serving dish, garnish with sprigs of watercress and serve immediately.

Wings of skate
with capers and blackbutter

4 fresh skate wings
1 onion
1 carrot
1 celery stick
bouquet garni
¼ pint white wine vinegar
salt
lemon and parsley for garnish

for the sauce:
6 oz clarified butter
capers to taste
chopped parsley
black pepper

Peel and thinly slice the onion, carrot and celery. Place in a pan large enough to cook the skate. Add two thirds of the wine vinegar, the bouquet garni and salt. Half fill the pan with cold water and add the wings of skate. Bring to the boil, then simmer for about 10 minutes over a low heat until the fish is cooked.

To make the sauce, melt the butter in a small frying pan and cook until golden brown. Add the remaining wine vinegar, capers, chopped parsley and black pepper to taste.

Drain the wings of skate and place on a serving dish. Pour the sauce over the fish and garnish with slices of lemon and parsley. Serve immediately.

Alfredo Restaurant
Conwy, Gwynedd

Proprietors B and L Ramicone
Chefs B and A Ramicone

Osso bucco

shank of veal (Ask the butcher to cut through the bone to give
    4 x 1 inch thick slices)
4 oz flour
4 fl oz olive oil
4 oz chopped onion
2 cloves garlic, crushed
2 tablespoons tomato purée
2 bay leaves
small sprig of fresh thyme
1 glass white wine
2 pints chicken stock
4 tomatoes
2 anchovy fillets
zest of ½ lemon
handful of fresh parsley
salt, pepper

Season the veal and roll in flour. Heat the oil in a casserole and sauté the veal until very brown on both sides. Remove the veal from the casserole and add the onions, garlic, tomato purée, herbs and 2 oz of flour to the casserole. (It is important to stir frequently as the mixture will easily stick to the pan). Sauté until medium brown. Add the wine and chicken stock, bring to the boil and season to taste. Add the veal and simmer. Slice the tomatoes, remove the seeds, chop roughly and add to the casserole. Place the lid on the casserole and cook in a moderate oven (Gas Mark 4, 350°F) for about 80 minutes.

Meanwhile, chop the anchovy fillets, lemon zest and parsley very finely. Sprinkle this mixture onto the casserole 5 minutes before serving.

Osso Bucco is a traditional Milanese dish usually served with pilaf rice. This is a useful dish for dinner parties as it can be taken straight from the oven to the table, but will not spoil if kept in a warm oven after the cooking time.

Mont Blanc

6 meringue shells, broken
1 large tin chestnut purée
1 pint double cream
1 oz icing sugar
1 tot of rum
12 ratafia biscuits (or small macaroons)
4 oz block dark chocolate
vanilla essence (optional)

Place the broken meringue shells in the centre of a cake board.

Beat a little vanilla essence into the chestnut purée if required. Mix ½ oz of the icing sugar into the chestnut purée. Heap the chestnut purée onto the meringue base.

Whip the cream with the rum and the remaining ½ oz of icing sugar. Put the mixture into a piping bag with a large star nozzle. Pipe the mixture over the chestnut purée in an irregular fashion, so that the whole thing looks like a mountain peak!

Place the ratafia biscuits or small macaroons around the base of the "Mont Blanc" and grate the chocolate over the whipped cream.

This sweet is delicious, but very rich. Small portions are recommended.

Gwesty Plas Maenan
Plas Maenan Hotel
Maenan, Llanrwst, Gwynedd

Proprietors Enid and Allan Wynne Jones

Suryn San Tudno
Saint Tudno sauce—for pork

½ pint white sauce (béchamel)
1 oz prawns
1 oz cockles
1 oz mussels
2 oz poached salmon (or other fish as available)
1 tablespoon fish stock
½ glass white wine
a little Worcestershire sauce
salt, pepper

Chop the seafood and fish. Add to the white sauce along with the fish stock. Simmer gently, adding the white wine. Season to taste. Serve hot.

This sauce is an ideal accompaniment to most cuts of pork, especially cutlets which have been boned and covered with breadcrumbs.

Wyau Môn
Anglesey eggs

1 lb leeks (or onions if leeks are out of season)
4 hard boiled eggs
½ pint white sauce (béchamel)
4 oz grated red cheese (e.g. Caws Llŷn)
salt, pepper
chopped parsley and lemon wedge for garnish

Clean and chop the leeks and cook for 10-15 minutes in boiling water. Strain and season. Arrange the leeks on the bottom of a large dish (or four individual dishes). Slice the eggs in half and place on the leeks. Add half of the cheese to the white sauce and pour over the eggs. Sprinkle with the remaining cheese. Brown under the grill.

Serve hot and garnished with a lemon wedge and chopped parsley.

This was once a popular Anglesey supper dish but originally potatoes would have been mashed with the leeks to make a more substantial base for the eggs and cheese sauce. This modified version of the dish is offered at Plas Maenan as a starter, and is a very easy dish to prepare at home.

Waterloo Motor Hotel
Betws-y-Coed, Gwynedd

Manager D N Nesbitt
Chef I M Jones

Coq au vin

4 legs of chicken (thigh and drumstick)
flour
salt, pepper
1 fl oz oil
12 button onions
2 oz button mushrooms
¼ lb lardons
½ pint Burgundy
sprinkle of herbs
garlic to taste
½ pint demi-glace sauce
fresh parsley for garnish

Flour and season the chicken legs and sauté in the oil in a frying pan. Cook for about 10 minutes until brown.

Place the chicken legs in a casserole. Brown the onions, mushrooms, and lardons in the remaining fat in the frying pan. Drain off the fat and add the wine, herbs, garlic and demi-glace. Pour this mixture over the chicken and cook for about 20 minutes.

Sprinkle with fresh parsley and serve with croûtons spread with pâté.

Recommended wine: Sidi Larbi (a full-bodied red wine from Morocco) or Bull's Blood

Kidneys Turbigo

1 ½ lb lamb kidneys
½ lb chipolata sausages
6 shallots
6 fl oz dry white wine
1 oz clarified butter
1 pint demi-glace sauce
salt
crushed black pepper
chopped parsley for garnish

Halve the kidneys, remove the skin and core. Soak the kidneys in cold water for a few minutes and then dry them.

Sauté the chopped shallots and kidneys in the clarified butter for a few minutes with black pepper. Season to taste. Drain off the fat. Add the wine and demi-glace and simmer for 10 minutes. Grill the chipolatas.

Serve the kidneys and chipolatas with pilaf rice. Garnish with chopped parsley.

Recommended wine: Chateau Talbot 1966

Eagles Hotel
Penmachno, near Betws-y-Coed, Gwynedd

Proprietors Mr and Mrs Munton
Chef Mrs Munton

Lentil soup

8 oz lentils
1 small onion
1 clove garlic
2 pints bone stock
salt, pepper
butter for frying

Boil the lentils in the stock until soft. Fry the chopped onion in a little butter. Liquidize the lentils in the stock and pour over the fried onion. Add the pressed garlic, salt and pepper. Simmer for 15 minutes.

Steak in wine

4 pieces stewing steak
½ pint red wine
1 pint bone stock
1 onion
1 clove garlic
2 bay leaves
3 cloves
salt, pepper
flour

Dip the steak in flour and seal in a hot frying pan. Place in a casserole with the wine, stock, chopped onion, crushed garlic, bay leaves and cloves. Season to taste. Cook in a very slow oven (Gas Mark 1, 275°F) for 2-3 hours until the meat is tender.

Castle Hotel
Bangor, Gwynedd

Bara brith

1 lb self-raising flour
8 oz Demerara sugar
8 oz raisins
2 cups cold tea
2 oz margarine or butter
1 egg
1 teaspoon mixed spice

Soak the sugar and raisins in the cold tea overnight.

Add the mixed spice to the flour and rub in the margarine. Beat in the egg and then stir the soaked raisins and sugar into the mixture.

Grease an oblong loaf tin and fill with the mixture. Bake in a pre-heated moderate oven (Gas Mark 4, 350°F) for about 1½ hours.

Serve sliced and buttered for afternoon tea.

Le Patron Restaurant
Wern Y Wylan
near Beaumaris, Anglesey, Gwynedd

Proprietor Bill Ashton

Gigot d'agneau à la maison

shank of lamb
3 fl oz olive oil
8 fl oz red wine
bay leaf
parsley
2 or 3 celery sticks
1 large onion
peppercorns
1 or 2 cloves garlic
8 oz carrots
1 parsnip (optional)
shallots
5 fl oz strong stock or double consommé

Bone and roll the lamb (to make it easier to carve). Marinate the lamb overnight or longer, in the olive oil, red wine, bay leaf, parsley, chopped celery, sliced onion, a few peppercorns and chopped garlic.

After marinating, add the peeled and chopped carrots, a few shallots, the stock and perhaps a parsnip.

Cook in a covered roasting dish in a warm oven (Gas Mark 3, 325°F) for 2½ hours, followed by 15 minutes on a roasting tray in a moderately hot oven (Gas Mark 6, 400°F). Serve the juice as gravy.

Suggested vegetables: (drained) leeks and roast or croquette potatoes.

Les pêches farcies

4 peaches
ground almonds
castor sugar
peach or apricot brandy
whipped cream
cocktail cherries and angelica for decoration

Carefully cut the peaches in half and remove the stones.

Fill the hollows with a soft mixture made from ground almonds and castor sugar moistened with brandy.

Top with whipped cream and decorate with half a cocktail cherry and a couple of slices of angelica.

Henllys Hall Hotel
Beaumaris, Anglesey, Gwynedd

Proprietor Val Williams

Welsh rarebit

1 onion
4 oz cheese
2 eggs
1 teaspoon dried mustard
2 tablespoons beer
1 dessertspoon brown sauce
4 slices buttered toast

Chop the onion and the cheese. Place them in a liquidiser with the eggs, mustard, beer and brown sauce and liquidize. Put the mixture into a saucepan and heat gently, stirring with a wooden spoon until it thickens.

Remove the crusts from the toast and place the mixture on the slices of toast. Place under the grill to brown.

Baked ham and parsley sauce

joint of uncooked ham
butter
mustard
crushed whole black pepper
salt
garlic
cloves
honey
¼ pint cider

for the parsley sauce:
2 oz margarine
2 tablespoons plain flour
½ pint milk
liquid from ham after baking
chopped parsley
pinch of mustard powder
1 teaspoon brown sugar
2 tablespoons fresh cream

Place the ham on a piece of foil. Spread with butter, mustard, a little garlic and seasoning. Stick a few cloves into the ham and spread honey over the top. Bring the foil around the ham, but before sealing pour the cider inside the foil. Seal and bake in a moderate oven (Gas Mark 4, 350°F). (Allow about 2 hours for a 4 lb joint).

To make the parsley sauce, melt the margarine, add the flour, heat and stir until honeycombed but not brown. Add the milk, stir and heat. Add the liquid from the ham and bring to the boil to form a moderately thick sauce. Add chopped parsley, the mustard powder and the brown sugar. Remove from the heat and before serving add the fresh cream.

Bulkeley Arms
Beaumaris, Anglesey, Gwynedd

Rösti

1 lb potatoes
2 oz butter

Boil the unpeeled potatoes in salted water for about 5 minutes. Cool them under running water for a few minutes. Drain and leave to stand for several hours.

Peel and grate the potatoes using a course grater. Heat the butter in a frying pan and when hot fry the shredded potato, pressing down firmly to form a large flat cake about 1 inch thick. Reduce the heat and fry gently until golden (about 10 minutes). Carefully turn the rösti over and cook the other side until golden.

Rösti can be served in place of the usual potato dish or for breakfast with fried eggs on top.

The Lobster Pot
Church Bay, Rhydwyn, near Holyhead, Anglesey, Gwynedd

Proprietor Gwynne Davies

Lobster Winterthur

1 x 4 lb live lobster

for the sauce:
6 oz butter
flour
1 glass dry white wine
⅓ pint milk
3 oz mushrooms, finely chopped
4 oz shrimps
1 tablespoon anchovy essence
salt, pepper

Place the lobster in boiling water and boil for about 20 minutes. (It will be killed almost instantly.) Cool quickly under running water. Lay the lobster on its back and remove the legs and claws. Split the whole shell down the middle with a sharp pointed knife. Discard the sacs in the head and the intestinal canal. Remove the meat and the coral from the shell, and the meat from the claws. Cut the meat into small pieces. Wash the shell and place the meat pieces and coral into the shell.

To make the sauce, melt 4 oz butter over a moderate heat and blend in enough flour to form a smooth paste. Add the wine and boil for a few minutes. Stir in the milk and cook for another 3 minutes.

In a separate pan, sauté the mushrooms in butter for 2 minutes. Add the shrimps and bring to the boil quickly. Add the anchovy essence and season to taste. Allow to cool.

Blend the mushrooms and shrimps into the sauce and pour over the whole lobster. Place under the grill for a few minutes to heat through.

Serve with green salad and garlic dressing.

Glantraeth
Trefdraeth, Bodorgan, Anglesey, Gwynedd

Proprietor J S Edwards

Menai Pride mussel pâté

8 oz cooked and shelled mussels
1 oz celery
1 oz carrot
1 oz breadcrumbs
2 oz herring roe
pinch of mixed herbs
pinch of dill weed
4 egg yolks
brandy and double cream to taste
pinch of crushed garlic
salt, pepper

Finely mince the mussels, vegetables and herring roe. Add the herbs, crushed garlic, breadcrumbs, salt and pepper. Bind well with the egg yolks, brandy and cream.

Cook in a bain-marie in a moderate oven (Gas Mark 4, 350°F) for 30 minutes.

Cool and serve with toast fingers.

Spare ribs in honey and cinnamon

pork spare ribs (4 ribs per person)
flour
salt, pepper
honey
ground cinnamon
lettuce and lemon for garnish

Pass ribs through seasoned flour. Soak the ribs in melted honey. Remove from the honey and cover liberally with ground cinnamon.

Place in a greased baking tin and cook in a slow oven (Gas Mark 2, 300°F) for 15-30 minutes, turning frequently.

Serve with lettuce and wedge of lemon.

Peach Snowdonia Range

1 Swiss roll
1 tin halved peaches
½ pint double cream
brandy
chocolate strands and cherries for decoration

Slice the Swiss roll, arrange on a serving dish and sprinkle with brandy. Place the peaches on top of the Swiss roll so that the dish looks like a range of mountains!

Whip some of the cream until it is fairly thick and not runny. Using a large spoon, pour the cream over the peaches. Place the dish in the refrigerator.

Before serving, whip the remaining cream until stiff and pipe around the dish. Decorate with chocolate strands and cherries.

Royal Victoria Hotel
Llanberis, Gwynedd

Manager G M Parry

Snowdon pudding

1 oz glacé cherries
4 oz raisins
4 oz shredded suet
4 oz fresh white breadcrumbs
1 oz ground rice
4 oz castor sugar
finely grated rind of lemon
2 large eggs — beaten
3 tablespoons marmalade
milk

Half fill a steamer or large pan with cold water and bring to the boil. Grease a two pint pudding basin and put a small round of greaseproof paper in the base.

Cut the cherries in half. Put a few of the cherries and raisins in the basin. Place the remaining cherries and raisins in a mixing bowl and add suet, breadcrumbs, ground rice, castor sugar and lemon rind. Mix in the beaten eggs and marmalade and add enough milk to give a soft, dropping consistency.

Spoon the mixture into the prepared basin. Cover pudding with a round of greaseproof paper and then with some aluminium foil.

Boil or steam for 2½ hours.

Serve with custard.

The Stables Restaurant
Plas Ffynnon, Llanwnda, Caernarfon, Gwynedd

Proprietors Richard and Jenny Howarth
Chef Hugh Jones

Stables strawberry gâteau

½ lb strawberries (or 15 oz tin)
¼ pint whipped cream
6 egg whites
12 oz castor sugar
2 oz flaked almonds

for the sponge:
4 oz self-raising flour
4 oz castor sugar
3 eggs

To make the sponge, whisk the castor sugar and eggs together until the impression of the whisk remains when the whisk is removed. Fold in the flour. Pour into a greased and floured 7 inch sponge tin. Bake in the centre of a moderately hot oven (Gas Mark 5, 375°F) for 25 minutes.

When the sponge is cold, slice in half. Place one half of the sponge on an oven-proof dish. Pile the strawberries and fresh cream on top. Place the other half of the sponge on top.

Whisk the egg whites until stiff. Add half the castor sugar and whisk again. Add the remaining 6 oz of castor sugar and whisk until the meringue is firm.

Either pipe the meringue over the gâteau or just roughly pile it over, making sure that the gâteau is sealed in by the meringue. Sprinkle with the almonds.

Bake in a moderately hot oven (Gas Mark 6, 400°F) for 15 minutes or until golden brown.

This gâteau can be served hot straight from the oven or cold. Do not place in a refrigerator as the meringue will lose its crispness.

Fresh orange with rum flavoured syrup

3 large oranges
¼ pint boiling water
¼ pint cold, boiled water
2 tablespoons sugar
2 tablespoons Jamaica rum

Peel the oranges and slice across into rings. Melt the sugar in the boiling water and, when completely dissolved, add the cold water. Add the rum to the syrup and then pour the syrup over the orange rings. When quite cold, place in the refrigerator.

For best results, prepare this sweet the night before to allow the rum time to soak into the fruit.

Serve with fresh cream.

The Dive Inn
Tudweiliog, near Pwllheli, Gwynedd

Proprietor Edric Williams
Chef Mary Williams

Aljotta — fish soup from Malta

for the fish stock:
1½ lb grey mullet or red bream
1 onion
1 wedge of lemon
salt, black pepper

for the sauce:
1 lb leeks
½ lb tomatoes (preferably tinned)
1 tablespoon tomato purée
chopped mint
3 celery sticks
1 medium sized potato
½ pint vegetable oil
1 clove garlic
chopped parsley and thyme for garnish

To make the fish stock, add the seasoning, onion and lemon to 2½ pints of water and bring to the boil. Add the fish, after de-scaling, and simmer for about 30 minutes.

Remove the fish from the stock and sieve the stock while the fish is cooling.

To make the sauce, chop the leeks and garlic and sauté in the oil. Add the tomatoes and the tomato purée and simmer for about 15 minutes. Add the mint, chopped celery and diced potato and cook for a further 15 minutes.

Bone and flake the fish and add to the stock. Add the prepared sauce and allow the soup to simmer over a low heat for about 30 minutes.

The soup must be served piping hot garnished with parsley and thyme.

Serve with thick slices of crusty brown bread.

Porth Tocyn Hotel
Abersoch, Gwynedd

Proprietors Mr and Mrs David Fletcher-Brewer
Head Chef Mrs M Brooks

Captain's relish

4 oz tuna fish
4 oz butter
1 clove garlic
2 teaspoons lemon juice

Beat all the ingredients together until smooth. Chill in a pâté dish in the refrigerator.

Serve with crisp toast fingers.

Norwegian style beetroot

3 medium sized beetroots
1 large cooking apple, cored and sliced
1 large onion, finely sliced
¼ pint soured cream
1 oz butter
pinch of cinnamon

Cook the beetroot in boiling salted water for approximately 25 minutes, until tender.

Meanwhile, fry the onion in the butter until transparent. Add the apple and cook for a further few seconds. Remove from the heat and drain.

Skin the beetroot when cooked and chop into rough dice. Add to the onion and apple mixture. Pour the cream over the mixture and reheat. Stir in the cinnamon and serve.

Roast loin of veal with lemon sauce

2 lb loin veal, boned (pork can be used instead of veal)
4 lemons
1 onion, chopped
sage
bacon strips
6 tablespoons Madeira (optional)
½ pint veal stock (make from bones the butcher will provide
   with the joint)
flour
salt, pepper
watercress and lemon twists for garnish

Trim the excess fat from inside the veal. If the kidney is still inside,
remove and cut up small. Grate two lemons. Spread the rind, the
chopped kidney, the chopped onion, a sprinkle of sage and salt and
pepper over the meat. Roll the meat and tie securely. Cover with bacon
strips and seasoning and place in a roasting tin. Squeeze over the juice
of three lemons and half the Madeira.

Cover the tin with foil and roast in a hot oven (Gas Mark 7, 425°F) for
about 45 minutes. When tender but not dry remove the meat and keep
warm on a serving tray.

The roasting pan juices are used to make the sauce. Add a little flour to
the juices and cook for a few minutes. Remove from the heat and add
the veal stock and the remainder of the Madeira. Thinly slice one lemon
removing the pips and add to the pan. Check the seasoning.

Serve the lemon sauce with the veal. Garnish with watercress and lemon
twists.

Damson and apple mousse

1 lb cooking apples
1 lb damsons
¼ pint water
4 oz castor sugar
juice of 1 lemon
½ oz powdered gelatine
2 egg whites

Peel, core and slice the apples into a saucepan. Add the washed and stoned damsons, the water and 3 oz of the sugar. Simmer for 15 minutes until the fruit is tender.

Meanwhile, leave the gelatine to soak in the lemon juice in a small basin.

When the fruit is cooked, remove from the heat, add the soaked gelatine and stir until dissolved. Put the fruit through a blender and set aside until cold and beginning to thicken. Pour a little of the fruit mixture into the bottom of a serving dish. Fold the beaten egg whites and 1 oz sugar into the remaining fruit mixture. Pour onto the purée and chill before serving.

Bronheulog Hotel
Abersoch, Gwynedd

Proprietor/Chef Stefano Zanier

Medallions of fillet of beef Campania

1 lb fillet steak
2 slices Parma ham or smoked ham
6 artichoke hearts
1½ lb peeled tomatoes
1 large onion
garlic
oregano
butter for frying

Chop the onion and fry until golden brown. Chop the tomatoes and mix with the onion. Add garlic according to taste and cook gently for 15 minutes. Finally, add oregano according to taste.

Slice the steak into medallions weighing about 2 oz each. Cut the artichokes into quarters.

Using another frying pan, fry the medallions in butter for 2 minutes. Remove the medallions from the pan and fry the artichokes.

To serve, place the ham on top of the medallions and the artichokes on the ham. Pour the tomato and onion mixture over the top.

Recommended wine: Valpolicella Bolla or Red Chianti.

Hotel Bryn Derwen
Llanbedrog, Gwynedd

Proprietor Patricia Blackburn

Pear and walnut salad

4 leaves from heart of lettuce
4 walnut halves
4 pear halves
4 teaspoons mayonnaise
4 teaspoons castor sugar

Using four saucer champagne glasses or small dishes, place one lettuce leaf in each glass. Place one pear half, cut side down, on each lettuce leaf and top with a teaspoonful of mayonnaise. Sprinkle castor sugar to taste on the mayonnaise and place a walnut half on top.

Chill in the refrigerator for a few minutes before serving.

Rabbit stew with claret

1 rabbit
8 small onions
4 oz bacon
1 pint stock
2 oz butter or dripping
2 oz plain flour
1 glass claret
bouquet garni
4 cloves
salt, pepper

Wash and joint the rabbit. Wash and dice the rabbit liver and put on one side.

Remove the rind from the bacon, dice and gently fry in fat until soft and lightly brown. Remove from the fat. Fry the sliced onions until soft and slightly brown and remove from the fat.

Fry the rabbit until lightly brown and remove from the fat. Add the flour to the fat to make a roux. Add the stock to the roux to make a sauce. Season well, add cloves and bouquet garni.

Place the rabbit portions, bacon and onions in the sauce. Cover the pan and simmer gently. After 45 minutes add the liver and stir in the claret. Gently simmer for a further 15 minutes until the rabbit is cooked. (It is important not to over-cook the rabbit, which should be young, tender meat.)

Serve with creamed potatoes and green vegetables.

Hotel Bryn Derwen

Banana trifle

1 plain Swiss roll (with raspberry or strawberry jam filling)
4 tablespoons sweet sherry
2 tablespoons raspberry or strawberry jam
1 lb bananas
1 lemon
1 oz castor sugar
½ pint double cream
angelica, flaked almonds and cherries for decoration

Thinly slice the Swiss roll and arrange over the base of a serving dish. Sprinkle with sherry and spread with jam.

Peel the bananas and squeeze the lemon. In a separate bowl, mash the bananas and mix well with lemon juice and sugar. Place in a layer over the Swiss roll mixture.

Whisk the double cream until thick and pour over the trifle just before serving.

Decorate with angelica, almond flakes and cherries.

This sweet should be made about half an hour before serving.

Villa Pandana
Garndolbenmaen, near Portmadoc, Gwynedd

Zuppa Inglese
Italian trifle

8 oz boudoir biscuits (sponge biscuits)
4 oz plain chocolate
drop of milk
1 wine glass Marsala or sweet sherry

for the custard cream:
½ pint milk
sugar
orange peel
custard powder
1 measure brandy or liqueur

To make the custard cream, mix the custard powder to a smooth paste with a little of the cold milk. Boil the remainder of the milk with the orange peel and sugar to taste. Strain off the peel before adding the custard powder. Add a measure of brandy or liqueur.

Melt the chocolate in a little milk over a low heat.

Cover the base of a deep serving bowl with a layer of the biscuits and sprinkle with some of the wine. Cover with a thin layer of the custard cream and then a thin layer of the melted chocolate.

Repeat two or three times, finishing with a layer of custard or chocolate.

Moelwyn Restaurant
Criccieth, Gwynedd

Proprietor/Chef Peter Booth

Kipper pâté

1 lb kipper fillets
3 oz butter
6 oz onion
1 teaspoon cayenne pepper
2 teaspoons mace
2 teaspoons lemon juice
1 glass medium dry white wine
4 eggs
pinch of sugar
½ teaspoon paprika
2 tablespoons cream
rashers of streaky bacon

for the white sauce:
1 oz margarine
1 oz flour
8 oz milk

Melt the butter in a pan, add the finely chopped onion and cook slowly. Skin the kipper fillets and add to the pan with the lemon juice, mace and cayenne pepper. Cover and cook for about 10 minutes. Remove from the heat and pass the mixture through a fine mincer or blend in a liquidiser until smooth.

To make the white sauce, melt the margarine, add the flour and allow to cook on a low heat for 2-3 minutes. Slowly add the milk.

Allow to cool, add the eggs and white wine and beat well. Stir in the kipper mixture, sugar, paprika and cream.

Line an earthenware terrine with streaky bacon and pour in the mixture. Cover with foil. Place in a bain-marie and cook for 1 hour in the centre of a moderately hot oven (Gas Mark 5, 375°F), removing the foil for the final 15 minutes. Leave weighted overnight, preferably in a refrigerator as it will be easier to turn out.

Place on lettuce leaves, garnish with parsley and a good wedge of lemon and serve with slices of brown bread or fingers of hot toast.

The Royal Goat Hotel
Beddgelert, Gwynedd

Gelert's pineapple

1 medium sized pineapple
1 orange
2 bananas
½ pint whipped cream
Kirsch or brandy

Cut off the top of the pineapple just below the spiky stem. Scoop out the inside of the pineapple without damaging the outer skin. Remove the hard core from the pineapple flesh.

Peel the orange, remove the pith and separate into segments. Roughly chop the pineapple flesh, bananas and orange.

Place the chopped fruit in a bowl, add the Kirsch or brandy and fold in the whipped cream.

Transfer this mixture into the pineapple shell and replace the top.

Chill in the refrigerator before serving on ice cubes.

The Saracen's Head Hotel
Beddgelert, Gwynedd

Chicken Royale

1 chicken, cut into four
flour
4 slices lean bacon
2 medium sized onions
2 green peppers
½ lb mushrooms
½ tablespoon mixed herbs
1 medium sized tin peeled tomatoes
¾ pint cider
3 tablespoons cooking oil
salt, pepper
¾ lb long grain rice

Coat the chicken in flour and season. Place the oil in a large casserole dish on medium heat. Fry the chicken in the oil for 2-3 minutes on each side.

Dice the bacon, slice the peppers and mushrooms and slice the onions into rings. Add the onion, bacon, peppers and herbs to the chicken. Place the lid on the casserole dish and sweat the contents for 15 minutes on low heat, stirring occasionally.

Add the mushrooms, tomatoes and cider. Stir lightly and bring to the boil. Place in a moderately hot oven (Gas Mark 5, 375°F) for 1½-2 hours.

Place the rice in 4 pints of salted boiling water and cook for 20 minutes. Strain and rinse well under cold water. Rinse again under boiling water 5 minutes before serving the meal. Cover the rice with melted butter, either garlic flavoured or plain.

Sygun Fawr Country House Hotel
Beddgelert, Gwynedd

Proprietors N and M Wilson

Dressed crab

1 medium crab
2 oz white breadcrumbs
1 teaspoon dry mustard
2 fl oz malt vinegar
salt, pepper
pinch of mace

Remove the meat from the crab's shell and scrub the shell clean. Blend the meat with all the seasonings and with the breadcrumbs. Replace in the shell and garnish.

Syllabub

1 lemon
3 oz castor sugar
3 tablespoons white wine
½ pint double cream

Peel the rind of the lemon finely and soak in the juice of the lemon and the white wine for 1½ hours.

Whisk the cream and sugar until stiff. Blend in the strained lemon juice and wine. Place in sundae dishes and decorate with a curl of lemon peel.

The Hotel Portmeirion
Penrhyndeudraeth, Gwynedd

Resident Director Michael Trevor-Williams
Chef Hefin Williams

Aubergines fourées

2 large aubergines
4 tomatoes, peeled and seeded
2 peppers
3 onions
3 cloves garlic
8 oz cooked ham
8 oz cooked rice
½ pint béchamel sauce
4 oz Parmesan cheese
salt, pepper
oil for frying

Cut open the peppers, remove the seeds and cut into thin slices. Fry gently with the sliced onion, tomatoes and garlic. When cooked, add the chopped ham and rice. Bind with a little of the béchamel sauce and season well.

Cut the aubergines in half lengthwise and remove the centres. Sprinkle with salt and leave for 15 minutes. Dry them and wipe off any excess salt. Fry each half in hot oil and then drain. Fill each aubergine half with the prepared mixture.

Arrange them in a fireproof dish and cover with the remaining béchamel sauce and the cheese. Place in a moderate oven, (Gas Mark, 4, 350°F) for 20 minutes. Serve very hot.

Recommended wine: Alsace — Dopff

Terrine de Sibier

1 pheasant
1 partridge
8 oz lean pork
8 oz duck or chicken livers
2 apples, peeled and cored
2 onions, sliced
2 cloves garlic
salt, black pepper
1 bay leaf, crushed
chopped parsley
teaspoon mixed spice
1 egg, well beaten
6 oz strips of pork fat or bacon

for the marinade:

1 onion, sliced
2 carrots, sliced
parsley stalks
1 bay leaf
1 clove garlic
chopped thyme
4 tablespoons brandy
4 tablespoons Madeira
¼ pint red wine

Skin and bone the pheasant and partridge. Place the meat in an earthenware or stainless-steel bowl with the onion, carrots, parsley, bay leaf, garlic and thyme. Pour on the brandy, Madeira and red wine. Leave to marinate overnight.

Pass the lean pork, livers, apples, onions, garlic and marinated meat through a medium grade mincer. Season with salt, ground black pepper, herbs and mixed spice. Stir in the egg and marinating liquid and mix well.

Cover the sides and bottom of an oven-proof terrine with strips of pork fat or bacon. Press in the mixture and top with more strips of pork fat. Place a lid on the terrine, place the terrine in a pan of hot water and bake in a moderate oven (Gas Mark 4, 350°F) for 90 minutes.

When cooked, remove the lid and place a weighted plate on top of the pâté to compress it. Allow two days before cutting. Serve with olives, gherkins and chopped aspic.

Recommended wine: Vougeot 1953 (Côte d'Or) Burgundy;
Mauro Daphne Merita — Greece
Delamain, Grand Champagne

Canneloni alla Vescovo

8 leaves canneloni
2 tablespoons olive oil
2 medium sized onions
2 cloves garlic
parsley
6 large tomatoes, peeled and seeded
1 tablespoon tomato purée
1 pint cooked mussels
4 oz peeled prawns
8 oz boiled monkfish
4 oz cooked shrimps
4 oz cooked and shelled cockles
1 pint béchamel sauce
4 oz grated Parmesan cheese
salt, pepper
oil for frying

Poach the canneloni leaves in salted boiling water to which the olive oil has been added. When cooked, remove and wash in cold water. Dry on a clean cloth.

Finely chop the onions, garlic and parsley. Slice the tomatoes. Fry the onions slowly in oil until golden brown. Add the tomatoes, garlic, parsley, tomato purée and a little water. Simmer gently for 5 minutes. Season and put aside.

Roughly chop the mussels, prawns, monkfish, shrimps and cockles. Add a little béchamel sauce and mix together.

Lay the pasta leaves flat. Divide the fish mixture into eight equal portions and place a portion on each leaf. Roll the leaves and place in an ovenproof dish. Pour the remaining béchamel sauce over the canneloni, sprinkle with the Parmesan cheese and pour the tomato mixture on top.

Cook in a moderately hot oven, (Gas Mark 5, 375°F) for 20 minutes.

Recommended wine: Corvo Salaparuta "Bianco" Castel Daccia (Palermo)

Bœuf des Marinieres

for 6 persons
3 lb beef, rump or fillet
6 fl oz olive oil
4 large onions
black pepper
salt
French mustard
4 oz anchovy fillets
bay leaf
2 cloves garlic
8 oz mushrooms
1 pint double cream
mixed herbs
parsley

Slice the meat thinly (about ¼ inch) and remove any fat or sinew. Finely chop the onion, garlic and anchovy fillets. Slice the mushrooms.

Fry the meat slices in the hot olive oil in a large casserole. Add the onions, salt, pepper and garlic and cook over a low heat for 10 minutes. Add the mushrooms, French mustard, anchovies, bay leaf, herbs and cream. Bring quickly to the boil, cover and place in a hot oven (Gas Mark 7, 425°F) for 15 minutes.

Serve with pilaf rice and boiled potatoes.

Recommended wine: Chateau Cos d'Estournel St. Estephe 1962 Bordeaux.

Bontddu Hall Hotel
Dolgellau, Gwynedd

Proprietor W S Hall
Manager R K Lewis
Chef Axel Arendt

Smoked haddock chowder

8 oz smoked haddock
milk
2 rashers bacon
1 large onion
4 or 5 medium sized new potatoes
garlic
black pepper
1 ½ pints fish stock
2 tablespoons double cream
chopped parsley

Poach the smoked haddock in milk. Reserve the juices. Flake the haddock free of bones and put to one side.

Blanch the diced bacon, chopped onion and diced potatoes with a little garlic and black pepper. Strain off the water. Add the fish stock and juices and simmer until the potato is cooked through. Add the haddock, remove from the heat and add the cream and chopped parsley. Check the seasoning (little or no salt should be required.)

Fried cheese stuffed mushrooms with devilled sauce

½ lb large mushrooms
3 oz grated Cheddar cheese
2 oz butter
2 oz flour
1 tablespoon milk
Tabasco
mustard
1 egg
breadcrumbs
oil

for the devilled tomato sauce:
1 cup tinned tomatoes
3 large skinned ripe tomatoes
1 teaspoon sugar
1 crushed clove garlic
2 tablespoons oil
1 dessertspoon vinegar
1 tablespoon Worcestershire sauce
1 dessertspoon tomato ketchup
salt, pepper, mustard

Remove the stalks from the mushrooms.

Melt the butter gently in a saucepan. Blend in the flour and stir over heat for a minute or two to make a white butter roux. Add the milk and grated cheese. Season with a little Tabasco and mustard.

Fill the mushroom caps with this cheese roux. Dip the stuffed mushrooms in beaten egg and coat in fresh white breadcrumbs. Deep fry.

To make the devilled tomato sauce, simmer the ingredients together for 25 minutes. Cool and liquidize, then re-heat before serving.

Bontddu Hall Hotel

Grilled Mawddach salmon en brochette with saffron rice and lemon butter sauce

1 salmon
salt, pepper
butter
4 oz long grain rice
saffron
cucumber and parsley for garnish

for the lemon butter sauce:
2 oz butter
1 oz flour
½ pint milk
juice of 1 lemon
salt, pepper
2 tablespoons cream

Fillet and skin the salmon. Cut into 1 inch cubes. Fix on skewers, season and butter well. Grill until just cooked through, buttering as grilling takes place.

To make the lemon butter sauce, melt 1 oz butter gently in a saucepan, belend in the flour and stir over heat for a minute or two to cook the flour. Add the milk, lemon juice and seasoning. Remove from the heat and stir in the cream and the remaining ounce of butter.

Remove the salmon pieces gently from the skewers onto a bed of saffron rice. (Add a pinch of saffron to the rice whilst boiling to flavour and colour.)

Garnish with cucumber and parsley. Serve the lemon butter sauce separately.

Pork fillet à la maison

1 ½ lb pork fillet
flour
2 eggs
1 tablespoon grated Parmesan cheese
salt, pepper
2 oz butter
8 oz spaghetti

for the sauce smitaine:
2 onions
2 oz butter
1 ½ cups sour cream
¼ pint dry white wine
salt, pepper

Trim any fat off the pork fillet and cut across into one inch pieces. Flatten slightly, coat in flour and dip into batter made from beaten eggs, grated Parmesan cheese and seasoning.

Fry gently in butter until cooked through and golden.

To make the sauce smitaine, fry the sliced onions in the butter until golden. Add sour cream and simmer for 20 minutes. Add wine. Sieve and season.

Serve the pork on a bed of buttered spaghetti with the sauce smitaine.

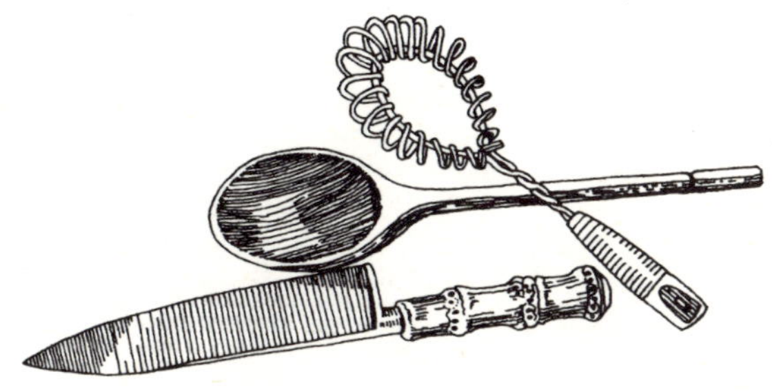

Cawl cennin Cymreig
Traditional Welsh cawl

1½ lb brisket for boiling
1½ lb shoulder of bacon for boiling
1½ lb potatoes
½ lb carrots
½ lb swede
½ lb parsnip
¼ lb dried peas, soaked
1 small cabbage
4 leeks
salt, pepper
3 pints water

Place the brisket and the bacon in a large saucepan with the water. Boil until tender but not quite cooked.

Peel the potatoes, carrots, swede and parsnip and slice into fairly large pieces. Wash and cut the leeks into large pieces. The cabbage leaves are used whole.

Add the carrots, swede, parsnip and peas to the meat and stock. Season to taste and cook for 15 minutes. Add the potatoes and cook for 10 minutes. Add the leeks and cabbage leaves and cook for a further 15 minutes.

The traditional way of eating cawl is to serve the stock, leek and cabbage in a basin as a first course, followed by the sliced meats served with the remaining vegetables (which can either be mashed with butter or eaten as served).

Recommended drink: mead

Trefeddian Hotel
Aberdovey, Gwynedd

Proprietor N J C B Cave
Chef George F Smith

Ice cream soufflé Grand Marnier

for 6 persons
3 eggs
2 oz castor sugar
½ pint double cream
2 teaspoons Grand Marnier
6 teaspoons chocolate vermicelli
or chocolate squares

Whip the eggs and sugar in a bowl over a pan of hot water until light and creamy and trebled in volume.

Whip the double cream until thick, then fold in the Grand Marnier. Gently fold the cream into the whipped eggs and sugar.

Prepare small, plastic soufflé dishes by tying a deep band of greaseproof paper around each dish so that the paper extends above the rim, doubling the depth.

Put the mixture into the prepared containers filling to well above the rim of the soufflé dish. Place in the freezer for 2 hours.

Remove from the freezer and take off the greaseproof paper. (The soufflés will appear to have risen.)

Serve the soufflés with chocolate squares or coated with chocolate vermicelli.

Ynyshir Hall
Eglwysfach, near Machynlleth, Powys

Proprietors Sam and Penny Roberts

Tomato Gervais

8 even sized tomatoes
3 dessertspoons hot milk
chopped chives
watercress or celery tops for garnish
8 oz Demi-sel cheese
salt, pepper

Cut the caps from the tops of the tomatoes. Using a grapefruit knife, remove the seeds and core and place them in a strainer.

Beat the cheese with the hot milk. Add salt and freshly ground black pepper, chives and a little of the strained tomato juice.

Fill the prepared tomatoes with this mixture and replace the caps.

Arrange on a serving dish and garnish with watercress or celery tops.

Venison in pastry

4 lb haunch of venison
1 ½ lb flour
water to mix
red wine
3 medium sized onions
sprig of thyme
parsley stalks
basil
marjoram
sage
salt
freshly ground black pepper

for the beurr-manié:
4 oz butter
4 oz flour

Make a pastry of the flour and water. Roll out and wrap around the haunch of venison, sealing the edges.

Place in a large casserole and pour in equal quantities of wine and water to come half way up the haunch. Add sliced onions, thyme, parsley stalks, basil, marjoram, sage, salt and black pepper. Leave to marinate in a warm atmosphere for 4 hours.

Cover with tin foil and cook in a moderate oven (Gas Mark 4, 350°F) for about 2 hours.

To make the beurre-manié, melt the butter in a pan and add the flour gradually. Allow flour to cook to make a smooth paste.

Strain off the liquid of the marinade and thicken with beurre-manié. Season to taste.

Remove pastry (this is not used) and the venison is ready to carve. Serve with the sauce.

Recommended wine: a Burgundy such as Vosne-Romanée

Conrah Country Hotel
Ffosrhydygaled, Chancery, near Aberystwyth, Dyfed

Proprietor R A Hughes

Casserole of veal

4 x 6 oz fillets of veal
2 large onions
4 skinned tomatoes
1 leek
2 oz mushrooms
4 large boiled potatoes
1 pint good stock
1 cup white wine
salt, pepper
garlic to taste
butter for frying
2 oz grated cheese

Beat the fillets until thin and cut into two or three pieces. Season well with salt, pepper and garlic. Lightly fry the veal in butter.

Chop the onions, tomatoes, leek and mushrooms and mix together. Slice the cold boiled potatoes.

Using a casserole dish for four portions, place a layer of the veal on the bottom and cover with a layer of the chopped ingredients. Repeat this procedure until all the veal is used. Cover the top with the sliced potatoes. Pour the stock and wine over the casserole and sprinkle with the grated cheese.

Cook in a moderate oven (Gas Mark 4, 350°F) for 45 minutes.

Suggested vegetables: new minted potatoes and garden peas

The Lamb Hotel
Rhos, Llangeler, near Llandysul, Dyfed

Proprietor P L, C M & K L Leighton
Head Chef K L Leighton

Chicken Maryland

4 chicken breasts
1 small tin sweet corn
2-3 tablespoons thick
 béchamel sauce
salt, pepper
flour
2 eggs
white breadcrumbs
oil for frying
butter
4 small tomatoes
4 bacon rashers
4 small bananas
parsley

for the horseradish sauce:
¼ pint cream
2 tablespoons grated horseradish
paprika
pinch of sugar
vinegar

Flatten the chicken breasts slightly. Dip them in flour, beaten eggs (having separated one egg yolk) and breadcrumbs.

Drain the sweet corn well and bind with the béchamel sauce. Add the egg yolk and season with salt and pepper. When this mixture is cold, shape into small, flat cakes. Dip them in the beaten eggs, coat with breadcrumbs and fry in hot oil.

Skin the bananas and halve lengthways. Sauté in butter. Grill the tomatoes.

Fry the chicken pieces in deep oil until they are golden brown (about 10 minutes). Fry the bacon.

Garnish the chicken with the corn fritters, tomatoes, bacon, bananas and parsley. Serve horseradish sauce separately.

To make the horseradish sauce, whip the cream, add the grated horseradish and season with paprika, a pinch of sugar and a few drops of vinegar.

Emlyn Arms Hotel
Newcastle Emlyn, Dyfed

Manager Richard A Hewlett

Whole grilled Teifi sewin with lemon and almond stuffing and cold cucumber sauce

4 sewin (8—10 oz each)
flour
butter

for the stuffing:
8 oz fresh breadcrumbs
1 lemon
2 oz chopped almonds
¼ oz sage
¼ oz chopped parsley
3 oz finely chopped onion
salt, pepper

for the sauce:
¼ pint double cream
4 oz cucumber
1 tablespoon white vinegar
salt, pepper

To make the stuffing, mix the breadcrumbs, almonds, sage, onion, parsley, salt and pepper, in a bowl. Grate the zest of the lemon into the bowl and add the juice of the lemon with sufficient water to bind the mixture.

Gut the fish and wash thoroughly. Fill with generous amounts of stuffing. Roll the fish in flour and place on a baking sheet. Coat with melted butter. Grill slowly for 15-20 minutes or until golden brown, turning once.

To make the cucumber sauce, chop the cucumber into cubes of not more than ¼ inch, and place in a bowl. Add the white vinegar, salt and pepper. Whip the double cream until stiff, add to the ingredients in the bowl and fold in.

Austrian coffee cake

6 oz butter
6 oz castor sugar
3 eggs
6 oz self-raising flour
salt
¼ pint strong black coffee
sugar
rum or brandy
½ pint whipped cream
vanilla essence

Cream the butter in a bowl. Add castor sugar, and cream again until light and fluffy. Beat in the eggs, a little at a time. Fold in the sifted flour with a pinch of salt.

Put the mixture into a 1½ pint ring mould or an 8 inch cake tin. Bake in a moderately hot oven, (Gas Mark 5, 375°F) for 25 minutes.

When cooked, remove from mould and set aside to cool. When cold, return to mould.

Sweeten the coffee to taste and flavour with the rum or brandy. Pour slowly over the cake whilst still in the mould. Turn out and mask with the whipped cream sweetened with sugar and flavoured with vanilla essence.

The Cliff Hotel
Gwbert-on-Sea, near Cardigan, Dyfed

Manager P Connor

French onion soup

12 oz shredded onions
2 oz butter
arrowroot or cornflour
3 pints brown stock (beef stock)
½ French loaf
salt, pepper
Parmesan cheese
2 oz chopped parsley for garnish

Melt the butter in a pan and fry the onions until well coloured. Add the stock and simmer for 20 minutes. Skim the grease, thicken with arrowroot and season to taste.

Slice the bread into rings and toast. Pour the soup into bowls and place the toasted bread on top. Sprinkle with Parmesan cheese and brown under the grill.

Garnish with the parsley.

Sewin and cucumber sauce

1 x 2 lb sewin
½ lemon
vinegar
salt

for the sauce:
½ cucumber, sliced thinly
1½ oz plain flour
1½ oz butter
2 tablespoons cream
¼ lemon
1 teaspoon Worcestershire sauce
1 pint milk
salt, pepper
2 oz fresh parsley for garnish

To make the cucumber sauce, melt the butter in a saucepan, add the flour and mix with a wooden spoon. Add the boiling milk a little at a time, stirring continuously. Add the cucumber, the Worcestershire sauce and the lemon juice. Season and simmer for 5 minutes.

Remove from the heat and stir in the cream.

To prepare the fish, add the juice of ½ lemon and a little vinegar to some boiling salted water in a shallow poaching pan. Place the fish in the pan and simmer for 10 minutes.

Remove the fish from the pan. Remove the skin from the body, leaving the head and tail natural.

Coat the body of the fish with the sauce, leaving the head and tail uncovered. Garnish with the fresh parsley.

Ferry Restaurant
St Dogmael's, near Cardigan, Dyfed

Mushrooms in garlic sauce

½ lb button mushrooms
1 clove garlic
¼ lb butter
salt, black pepper
4 slices toast
chopped parsley for garnish

Wash and peel the mushrooms. Melt the butter in a pan with the
crushed garlic, salt and black pepper to taste. Add the mushrooms and
cook for about 5 minutes.

To serve, cut the crusts from the pieces of toast. Cover the toast with the
mushrooms and sauce. Garnish with chopped parsley.

Ye Old Salutation Inn
Velindre, Crymych, Dyfed

Proprietor Joan Voyce
Chef Alan Jones

Salutation lobster

4-6 lb live lobster
¼ pint vinegar
1 pint white sauce
4 tablespoons dry white wine
4 tablespoons fresh cream
2 oz butter
lemon juice
salt, pepper
paprika
Parmesan cheese

Plunge the live lobster into boiling salted water with the vinegar. Boil for about 20-25 minutes. Leave to cool in the cooking liquor.

When cool, cut the lobster in half lengthways. Remove the claws and legs. Remove all the white meat, using a small hammer to break open the claws, legs and tail.

Cut the meat into mouth-size pieces and add to the white sauce. Bring to the boil and add the wine, a few drops of lemon juice, the butter, salt, pepper, a little paprika and the cream.

Clean and wash the two halves of the shell. Place the sauce containing the lobster meat into the shells. Sprinkle with Parmesan cheese and place under a hot grill until golden brown.

Suggested vegetables: garden peas, asparagus, new or creamed potatoes

Fishguard Bay Hotel
Fishguard, Goodwick, Dyfed

Salmon steak Lady Jane

4 salmon steaks
flour
butter for frying
8 oz uncooked white fish
 (cod, haddock, whiting etc)
4 oz prawns
4 oz artichoke hearts
1 egg white
salt, pepper
hollandaise sauce
green asparagus for garnish

Flour and season the salmon steaks. Cook very gently in butter until half cooked (about 5 minutes). Cut out the bone.

To make the forcemeat, finely chop the white fish after removing the bones. Fold in the chopped prawns, chopped artichoke hearts, whisked egg white and seasoning. Mix thoroughly. Fill the recess in each salmon steak with the forcemeat. Finish cooking in a moderate oven, (Gas Mark 4, 350°F).

To serve, coat the forcemeat with hollandaise sauce and garnish with asparagus.

Braised lettuce with cucumber sauce

2 lettuces
butter
salt, pepper
¼ pint stock
chopped parsley and chives for garnish

for the cucumber sauce:
1 oz butter
1 oz flour
¾ pint milk
1 onion
3 cloves
1 small cucumber, grated
salt, pepper

To make the cucumber sauce, heat the milk to boiling point with the
onion stock with the cloves. Allow to stand for 30 minutes and then
remove the onion. Melt the butter in a saucepan, add the flour and
cook for a few minutes without browning. Add the milk stirring
continuously until a creamy sauce is formed. Cook for 3 minutes. Add
the grated cucumber and simmer for 5 minutes, stirring occasionally.
Check the seasoning.

To prepare the braised lettuce, boil the whole lettuces in salted water for
5 minutes. Drain then squeeze in a dry cloth to remove all the water.
Cut each lettuce in half, mould each half into an oval shape and lay on a
baking tray. Season with salt and pepper and brush with butter. Add the
stock and cover with tin foil. Bake in the oven for 15 minutes.

To serve, pour the cucumber sauce over the braised lettuce and sprinkle
with freshly chopped parsley and chives.

Plas Glyn-y-Mel
Lower Fishguard, Dyfed

Proprietors Lt Colonel and Mrs F H Blofeld
Chef Mrs Blofeld

Grapefruit cocktail

2 grapefruit
4 oz picked shrimps
¼ pint double cream
1 clove garlic
curry powder
4 red cocktail onions for garnish

Cut the grapefruit in half across the segments. Carefully cut round the skin to loosen each segment. Place the segments in a strainer over a basin. Clean the grapefruit shells by removing the pithy centre and the skin from between the segments. Place the shells in grapefruit glasses.

Whip the cream lightly in a bowl which has been previously rubbed with the garlic clove. Blend in a teaspoonful or two of juice from the drained fruit and a little curry powder to taste.

Marinade the shrimps in this for an hour or two and then stir the grapefruit sections into the mixture.

Serve the mixture in the grapefruit shells. Garnish each shell with a cocktail onion. Serve cool, but not too cold as this would impair the flavour.

Green beans Chinese style

1 lb green beans
2 rashers streaky bacon
1 root fresh ginger
salt, pepper

Cut the bacon into small pieces and heat in a frying pan to extract the bacon fat. Add the ginger and green beans to the pan, turning over two or three times in the fat. Choose a lid a little too small for the pan. Place the lid over the beans, ginger and bacon and pour in about ½ pint of water. Cook gently until the water disappears. Remove the lid and season to taste.

Green beans Chinese style is a novel way of preparing this popular vegetable and can be served with a variety of dishes.

Whitesands Bay Hotel
Whitesands, St David's, Dyfed

Proprietor J R Watts-Evans

Escalopes sauté oriental with egg fried rice

4 oz fillet steak
4 oz pork fillet
breasts of one 3 lb chicken
1 large onion
1 red pepper
6 mushrooms
1 carrot
1 stick of celery
4 oz bamboo shoots
1 clove garlic
1 chillipepper
pinch of rosemary
½ oz flour
5 fl oz red wine
juice of ½ lemon
olive oil for frying
salt, black pepper

Cut the onion, peppers and mushrooms into thick slices. Split the carrot lengthwise and cut the bamboo shoots and celery into ⅛ inch thick pieces. Crush the garlic.

Cover the bottom of a large frying pan with a thin layer of olive oil, heat until a haze appears, then add the onion, carrot and garlic. Sauté for 2 minutes, turning frequently, then add the rest of the vegetables and rosemary. Sauté on a medium heat, turning frequently, until cooked. Sprinkle the flour over the mixture and mix in. Add the wine, lemon juice, salt and pepper to taste and bring to the boil. Place on one side to keep warm.

Cut the meats into slices a ¼ inch thick. Season with salt and freshly ground black pepper.

Heat a thin layer of olive oil in a sauté pan until smoking. Add all the meats and sauté quickly until brown. Reduce the heat and cook slowly until done. Drain off any oil left, mix the meats with the vegetables and bring to the boil.

Serve very hot with egg fried rice.

for the egg fried rice:
8 oz long grain rice
salt, pepper
oil for frying
1 egg

To make the egg fried rice, boil the long grain rice in salted water until just done. Wash and drain well. Heat a little oil in a frying pan. Add the well seasoned beaten egg and stir quickly with a fork, so that as the egg sets, it breaks up. Add the rice immediately and cook over a strong heat, turning continuously.

It is important not to over-cook the vegetables. They must be crisp so as to retain their individual flavours and colour and provide a contrast in texture to the meats which should be very tender.

Recommended wines: Charmes Chambertin or Lacrima Christi Bianco

Schwarzwalder kirschtorte
Black Forest gâteau

Serves 10-12 portions

8 oz sugar
2 oz flour
1 ½ oz cocoa
3 oz sponge crumbs
3 oz ground almonds
9 eggs
1 lb black cherries, pitted
2 pints cream
cornflour
3 fl oz Kirsch
grated chocolate and cherries for decoration

Separate the yolks from eight of the eggs and beat with the remaining whole egg, the sugar and a tablespoon of warm water. Add the ground almonds and the sponge crumbs. Fold in the stiffly beaten egg whites and then the sieved flour and cocoa. Place the mixture in a greased and floured 10 or 12 inch cake tin. Bake in a moderately hot oven, (Gas Mark 5, 375°F) for about 25 minutes.

When cold, slice into three layers. Cover the bottom layer with the cooked cherries bound with a little cornflour and 1 oz of the Kirsch.

Place the second layer on top and cover with Kirsch flavoured whipped cream. Repeat with the third layer. Cover the sides with cream and decorate with piped cream, grated chocolate and cherries.

Proprietor P A Trier

Carrot and tomato soup

8 oz peeled sliced carrots
12 oz skinned tomatoes (or tinned tomatoes)
½ pint chicken stock (or stock cube and water)
I bay leaf
basil or tarragon
Worcestershire sauce
margarine
salt, black pepper

for garnish:
finely chopped parsley
or grated raw carrot
or cream

Fry the carrots in margarine for about 3 minutes. Add the chicken stock, bay leaf, a sprinkle of basil or tarragon, a dash of Worcestershire sauce and a big pinch of salt and pepper. Simmer until the carrots are tender. Add the tomatoes and simmer for another 5 minutes. Remove the bay leaf and liquidize.

Garnish with a sprinkle of chopped parsley or grated raw carrot or with a teaspoonful of cream.

Cartref Restaurant

Beef casseroled in cider
with apples and parsley

2 lb beef (rump or round)
1 pint cider (sweet or dry to taste)
1 lb cooking apples
6-8 sprigs fresh parsley
¼ lb mushrooms
2 medium sized onions
juice of ½ lemon
Worcestershire sauce
flour
oil
2 chopped cloves garlic
salt, pepper
French mustard

Cut the meat into cubes and place in a dish with the cider, half of the parsley (finely chopped), garlic, salt, pepper and French mustard. Mix thoroughly and leave to marinate in the refrigerator for at least 24 hours, turning about every 8 hours.

Remove the meat from the marinade. Fry in a little oil and coat in flour. Chop and fry the onions. Chop two of the apples (which need not have been peeled). Put these apples, the onions and beef into a casserole. Add the remainder of the parsley, the lemon juice, salt, pepper, Worcestershire sauce and French mustard to taste.

Cover with the marinade and boiling water. Bring to the boil and cook in a moderate oven (Gas Mark 4, 350°F) for about 2 hours. (The exact timing will depend on the tenderness of the meat and on how long it has been marinating. It should eventually be tender but not flaking and tasteless — the only sure way is to try a piece after the first hour and a half).

Shortly before serving, chop the mushrooms and the remaining apples and add them to the casserole. They should both become hot, but on no account allowed to become mushy. Adjust seasoning, and thicken with cornflour if necessary.

Serve with any fresh, simple vegetables — carrots and cabbage are particularly suitable. Alternatively, be informal and serve with plenty of home baked bread to soak up the gravy.

Fresh pineapple and peaches in rum

1 fresh pineapple
3 fresh peaches
2 measures (1 miniature) dark or white rum

for decoration:
maraschino cherries
or mint
or angelica etc

Cut top off pineapple and scoop out all the fruit, taking care not to cut the skin. Chop the pineapple flesh and the peaches and mix thoroughly. Pour rum over the mixture. Leave in the refrigerator for 8-12 hours, turning occasionally.

Pile into the pineapple shell and decorate with maraschino cherries, mint, angelica etc.

For a really rich variation, use dark rum and add a little powdered ginger and 2 or 3 teaspoons of brown sugar.

For a much lighter version, use white rum and add some chopped mint and a little lemon juice.

It would be possible to use tinned fruit, although the decorative effect of the pineapple shell would be lost. In this case do not add any sugar as the syrup from the tins is sweet enough already, in fact, it may help to add a little lemon juice to give it a slight tang.

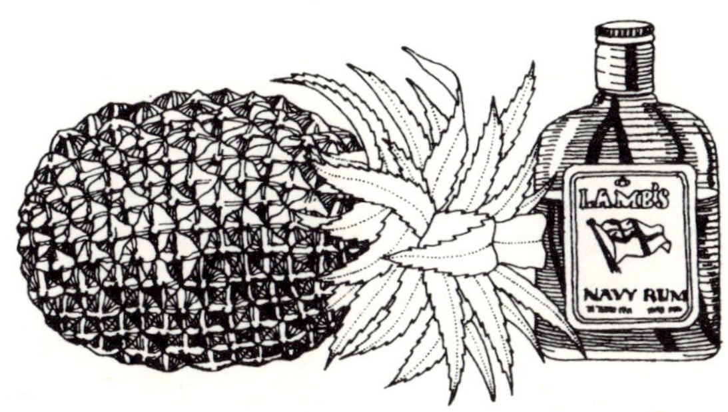

**Warpool Court Hotel
St David's, Dyfed**

Proprietors Grahame, David and Robert Lloyd
Co proprietor in charge of kitchens Grahame Lloyd
Chefs Michael Selwyn and David Murphy

Chicken Gujarat

1 chicken (about 4 lb)
1 large onion, finely chopped
salt, pepper
2 teaspoons cumin
2 teaspoons turmeric
4 oz butter
4 oz flour
2 pints chicken stock
1 tin apricots

Quarter the chicken and pass the joints through seasoned flour.

Melt the butter in a pan and fry the chicken portions and onion until golden brown. Remove the chicken and onion from the pan. Add the cumin, turmeric and flour to the butter left in the pan to form a roux. Cook slowly for 2-3 minutes. Add the chicken stock to make the sauce.

Use half the tin of apricots to make a purée. (Reserve the remainder of the apricots whole for garnish.) Add the apricot purée to the sauce. Replace the chicken in the sauce and cook for about 45 minutes. Check the seasoning.

Serve on a bed of rice and garnish with whole apricots.

Cheese-cake with Kirsch

for 6-8 persons

4 oz butter
1 packet digestive biscuits
1 lb pineapple
1 lemon
1 lb cottage cheese
¾ pint double cream
2½ leaves gelatine (about ¼ oz)
2 egg yolks
4 oz castor sugar
1 measure Kirsch

Crush the biscuits and melt the butter. Stir the biscuits into the butter, place in a 6 inch baking tin and press down evenly with a wooden spoon.

Soften the gelatine in the Kirsch and then dissolve over a very low heat. Allow to cool.

Press the cheese through a fine mesh into a mixing bowl. Whip the cream and fold into the cheese (reserving a little of the cream for decoration). Add the egg yolks, the sugar, the finely grated peel of the lemon and the juice of the lemon.

When the gelatine is cold but not set, add to the other ingredients in the bowl and mix thoroughly.

Dice the pineapple into cubes, drain well and add to mixture, (reserving about 4 oz of the pineapple for decoration).

Place the mixture on top of the biscuit base and set in the refrigerator. Decorate with rosettes of piped cream and small pineapple cubes.

St Non's Hotel
St David's, Dyfed

Proprietor Andrew M Stirling
Chef Rosanna Lloyd

Scallops maison

8 large scallops
8 long rashers streaky bacon
salt, pepper

for the hollandaise sauce:
2 egg yolks
4 oz butter cut in small pieces
salt, pepper
1 tablespoon white wine vinegar

Cut the scallops in half and season. Cut each rasher of bacon in half and wrap the halved scallops inside the bacon pieces. Secure them on skewers, four to each skewer.

Grill for 5 to 7 minutes until the bacon is crispy. Do not overcook or they will go tough.

To make the hollandaise sauce, whisk the vinegar, egg yolks and seasoning together in a bowl set over hot water until the sauce begins to thicken. Stir in the butter pieces gradually but do not allow to boil or it will curdle. When the sauce is thick it is ready to serve.

Place the scallops on a serving dish and coat with the hollandaise sauce.

Place under the grill for a few seconds until the sauce has a golden brown glaze. Serve with rice.

Recommended wine: Bourgogne Aligoté 1972

Ham and asparagus soufflé

1 small tin of green asparagus
¼ lb cooked ham
salt, pepper, nutmeg, mace
2 eggs

for the béchamel sauce:
½ pint milk
1 small onion
4 peppercorns
salt
¾ oz butter
¾ oz flour
1 small carrot
½ small celery stick
1 sprig parsley
2 cloves

To make the béchamel sauce, cut the onion into quarters, slice the carrot thickly and break the celery into 2 or 3 pieces. Add these vegetables to the milk, parsley, cloves and seasoning. Bring slowly to the boil, stirring all the time. Remove from heat and leave for 5 minutes. In a separate saucepan, gently melt the butter, stir in the flour to make a white butter roux and cook for two minutes. Separate the milk and vegetables by pouring the mixture through a sieve. Gradually blend the milk into the roux. Bring to the boil stirring continuously whilst it thickens, and simmer for 5 minutes.

Place the ham, asparagus with the juice from the tin and the béchamel sauce in a liquidiser and blend. Pour into a bowl and add the seasoning to taste. (Add a little extra salt as the soufflé will be increased in quantity by the egg whites.) Mix in the yolks and then gently fold in the stiffly beaten egg whites.

Put into 4 buttered ovenproof dishes or ramekins and bake in a hot oven (Gas Mark 6, 400°F) until well risen.

Recommended wine: Bourgogne Aligoté 1972

Pheasant poivrade

2 pheasants
6 rashers bacon
1 large carrot
½ large onion
3 cloves garlic
1 stick celery
3 or 4 juniper berries
2 glasses red wine
½ pint good brown stock
bay leaf
2 teaspoons black pepper
salt
chopped parsley

for the beurre-manié:

1 oz butter
1 oz flour

Roast the pheasants, covered with the bacon and cooking foil, in a moderate oven (Gas Mark 3, 325°F) for 1½ to 2 hours until moist and cooked.

When they are ready, tip off the juices into a thick bottomed saucepan and put the bacon to one side. Reduce the juices until they are burning in the base of the pan. Pour off the fat that is left. Into this pan put the onion, garlic, bacon, carrot, celery, all finely chopped. Stir over a high heat until the vegetables have soaked up the juices from the base of the pan. Simmer for a few minutes and add the wine, stock, juniper berries, bay leaf and pepper. Simmer again for 10 minutes.

To make the beurre-manié, melt the butter and add the flour gradually. Allow the flour to cook to make a smooth paste.

Add the beurre-manié in small quantities to thicken the sauce. Add salt to taste.

Split the pheasants in half and pour the sauce over them. Sprinkle with chopped parsley.

Suggested vegetables: Red cabbage and sprouts, creamed and baked potatoes.

Recommended wine: Fleurie 1972

Fraises Marquise

1 lb strawberries
Kirsch
12 fl oz double cream
4 oz sugar
4 oz castor sugar

Soak half the strawberries in Kirsch for about an hour. Mash the remaining strawberries, or if possible purée in a liquidizer.

Whip the cream with the 4 oz of sugar and add to the puréed strawberries.

Pile into small glass dishes.

Remove the strawberries from the Kirsch, roll them in the castor sugar and arrange on top of the cream.

Recommended wine: Champagne

Cuffern Hotel
Roch, near Haverfordwest, Dyfed

Proprietor G Barath

Chateaubriand with chasseur sauce

Chateaubriand is a thick steak cut from the middle of the head of the
fillet. It is the most tender and best flavoured among the steaks and
can be served with a selection of vegetables.

for the chateaubriand:

2 lb fillet steak
salt, pepper
½ oz butter
4 croûtons (small thin slices of bread)
fat for frying
8 artichoke bottoms
12 asparagus spears
2 tomatoes
8 oz sweet corn
8 oz mushrooms
8 oz croquette potatoes (mashed potatoes formed into fingers, coated
    in seasoned flour, beaten egg and breadcrumbs and fried until crisp
    and brown)

for the chasseur sauce:

1 oz butter
½ oz chopped shallots
2 oz sliced mushrooms
⅛ pint dry white wine
¼ lb tomatoes, roughly chopped
½ pint demi-glace sauce
chopped parsley and tarragon

Grill the fillet steak and sprinkle with salt and pepper. Add the butter to the fillet.

Prepare all the vegetables. Fry the croûtons in shallow fat until brown on both sides.

Cook the vegetables and arrange around a serving plate. Place the croûtons in the centre of the plate.

When the meat is cooked, cut into slices ⅛ inch thick and place over the croûtons. Serve with the chasseur sauce.

To make the chasseur sauce, melt the butter in a small frying pan, add the shallots and cook gently for 2-3 minutes without colouring. Add the mushrooms, cover with a lid and cook gently for 2-3 minutes. Strain off the fat.

Add the wine and reduce by half. Add the tomatoes and the demi-glace. Simmer for 5-10 minutes.

Check the seasoning and add the tarragon and parsley.

Druidstone Hotel
Druidston Haven, near Haverfordwest, Dyfed

Proprietors/Chefs Rod and Jane Bell

Scallops à la crème

16 large fresh or frozen scallops
10 spring onions
4 tomatoes
Irish whiskey for flaming
salt, pepper
freshly chopped parsley
⅓ pint cream
butter for frying
flour

If using fresh scallops in the shell, place them in a hot oven for 2 or 3 minutes until they open. The white scallop flesh and the orange roe are the parts used in this dish; dispose of the black frill around the white flesh.

Chop the spring onions and the skinned and deseeded tomatoes. Fry gently in a little butter and set aside. Lightly toss the prepared scallops in seasoned flour. Place in the pan and fry gently for a few minutes. Flame with a little Irish whiskey. Add the spring onions, tomatoes, cream, salt, pepper and parsley. Shake the pan and turn the ingredients carefully until the dish 'comes together'.

Serve in the scallop shells.

Suggested vegetables: New potatoes and green salad.

Recommended wine: Gewurztraminer

Fresh strawberry and melon flan

for the pastry:

8 oz plain flour
4 oz butter
4 oz castor sugar

for the filling:

2 punnets strawberries
1 small melon
½ lb red-currant jelly
sugar

Make the pastry in the usual way. Roll out and prepare a flan case. Bake blind until the pastry is lightly coloured. Allow to cool.

To prepare the filling, cut the melon flesh into cubes or scoop into balls. Lightly sugar and set aside in a sieve to allow the juice to seep through. This should take about 20-30 minutes. Mix this melon juice with the red-currant jelly and reduce slightly over a gentle heat, (test by putting a spoonful on a cold plate — if it sets, It is ready.)

Arrange the strawberries and melon in the flan case and glaze with the red-currant mixture.

Recommended wine: Chateau Rieussec

Chez Gilbert Restaurant
Pembroke House Hotel
Haverfordwest, Dyfed

Proprietor Gilbert Jean Lacroix

Lapin façon paysanne
Rabbit peasants style

1 rabbit (2¼ — 2¾ lb)
4 streaky rashers of bacon
1 onion
1 tablespoon English mustard
4 apple halves
1 egg-cupful olive oil
1 clove garlic
salt, pepper
1 glass white wine
2 glasses water

Gently sauté the whole rabbit in a baking pan for 20 minutes until lightly brown on most parts. Pull the legs apart slightly and press down to allow the inside of the legs to fry as well.

Cut the rabbit into four and season. Place in a pan, add the chopped onion and bacon and stir well. Place in a moderate oven (Gas Mark 4, 350°F) for 45 minutes.

Remove from the oven and strain off the fat. Spread the mustard, chopped garlic and olive oil all over the rabbit. Add the four apple halves, the wine and the water and replace in the oven until cooked, which should not take more than 15 minutes. Baste well when removing from the oven.

Serve with well drained spinach sauté and croquette potatoes.

Recommended wine: Mouton Cadet Bergerie 1970

Coach House Inn
Pembroke, Dyfed

Proprietor/Chef David Waters

Chilli con carne

½ — 1 lb beef, diced
8 oz red kidney beans
2 oz butter
oil
2 oz onion
2 oz bacon
1-2 cloves garlic
chilli powder (1 teaspoon — 1 dessertspoon to taste)
salt, pepper
2 oz tomato purée

Simmer the kidney beans in 3 pints of water for 1 hour. Allow the beans to cool in the water for 1 hour.

Heat the butter and a little oil in a frying pan. In this, sweat the chopped onion, crushed garlic and diced bacon. Remove and place in a casserole dish.

Sauté the diced beef in the flying pan and place in the casserole dish.

Mix the tomato purée and chilli powder and salt and pepper to taste with ½ pint of water. Simmer for a few minutes. Add to the casserole. Simmer for 2-3 hours.

Drain the beans and mix into the cooked casserole, which is then ready for serving.

For a really cheap meal use less meat and more beans.

The Royal Gate House Hotel
Tenby, Dyfed

Sole fourée

4 x 14 oz Dover soles
breadcrumbs
3 eggs
oil for frying
lemon and parsley for garnish

for the sauce:

8 oz prawns
4 oz butter
½ pint white wine
½ pint double cream

Skin both sides of the Dover soles leaving tails on. On one side make an incision both sides of the bone, about 3 inches long. By working a sharp knife inside the fish, following the bone to a depth of one inch on both sides, fold back giving an open purse effect.

Coat the fish all over in egg and breadcrumbs and deep fry.

To make the sauce, gently fry the peeled prawns in the butter and white wine. When the wine has reduced, add the double cream and heat gently until it thickens. Pour over the centre of the fish.

Serve on a dish paper on a serving plate. Garnish with lemon and parsley.

Buckingham Hotel
Tenby, Dyfed

Proprietor/Chef Geoffrey Greasley

Noisettes of lamb Dinbych

1 saddle new season Prescelly lamb
4 whole lamb kidneys
2 oz mint leaves
2 oz clarified butter
2 tomatoes for garnish

for the beurre noisette:
2 oz soft butter
salt, pepper

for the pancakes:
8 oz cooked sweet corn
2 egg yolks
2 oz flour
2 oz red-currant jelly
2 oz oil for frying

Remove the bones from the meat and cut in half lengthways. Insert the mint leaves and roll up tightly, tying with string. Divide into eight equal portions, two per person. Slit the kidneys lengthways but do not cut in half. Pin them open with wooden cocktail sticks. Fry the lamb portions and kidneys gently in the clarified butter until well coloured.

To make the pancakes, mix all the pancake ingredients together. Mould into eight rounds, approximately the same size as the lamb, and fry in the oil.

Remove the string from the lamb and the cocktail sticks from the kidneys. Place the kidneys on top of the lamb portions and place each lamb portion on a pancake. Garnish with half a tomato grilled.

To make the beurre noisette, place the soft butter in a hot frying pan, allow to turn brown and season. Pour over 'the dish' and serve immediately.

Suggested vegetables: Pommes rissolés (boiled new potatoes tossed in butter) and haricots verts niçoises (fresh whole green beans with tomato and garlic).

Malin House
Saundersfoot, Dyfed

Scampi Provençale

scampi
lemon juice
butter for frying

for the sauce:
1 tablespoon chopped onion
1 clove crushed garlic
1 green pepper, de-seeded and chopped
1 red pepper, de-seeded and chopped
1 tablespoon chopped mushrooms
1 lb tin peeled tomatoes
½ teaspoon sugar
1 dessertspoon tomato soup powder
salt, black pepper
oil and butter for frying

To make the sauce, fry the onion, garlic, peppers and mushrooms in a little butter and oil in a saucepan until tender but not coloured. Whisk the tin of tomatoes and add to the pan. Continue cooking and stirring until all the ingredients are blended together. Add the ½ teaspoon of sugar. Thicken the sauce with a dessertspoon of tomato soup powder dissolved in a little water. Season to taste.

Fry the required number of scampi in butter and lemon juice. Serve on a bed of plain boiled rice with the hot sauce poured over the scampi.

Lemon mousse

2 pints vanilla ice cream
½ pint single cream
6 oz lemon jelly crystals

In a saucepan, warm the single cream to approximately body temperature, then add and dissolve the jelly crystals. Remove from the heat.

Allow the ice cream to soften. Whisk in a cake-mixer using a wire whisk. When the ice cream has increased in volume by 50% pour it into the prepared cream and jelly. Mix and thoroughly blend together. Pour into moulds and leave to set in the refrigerator.

To demould, place the mould in hot water for a second and turn onto a serving dish.

This mousse can be used as a filling for Charlotte Russe, Ice Bombes or Gateau St Honore, or is delicious served by itself.

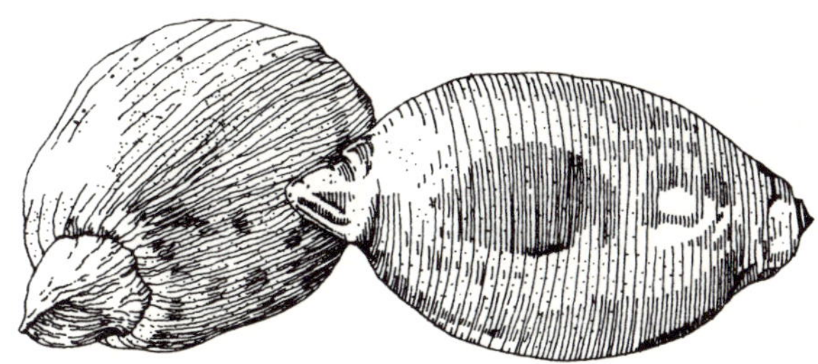

Robeston House
Robeston Wathen, near Narberth, Dyfed

Pork with apricot and almonds

joint of pork for roasting
½ lb dried apricots
2 oz almonds
1 large onion
½ pint Marsala wine
½ oz butter
2 oz fresh breadcrumbs
salt, pepper

Add enough boiled water to cover the apricots and soak for 1 hour.

Finely chop the onion and sauté in the butter until soft. Add the softened apricots, roughly chopped, with a little of the liquid in which they have been soaking. Add the Marsala and season. Add the almonds and mix in the breadcrumbs.

Use this mixture to stuff the joint of pork and roast in the usual way.

This recipe can be used to make a sauce if the breadcrumbs are omitted and more liquid is added. If necessary the sauce can be thickened at the end with a little cornflour.

Orange gâteau

1 plain 8 inch sponge
1 tin mandarin oranges
1 pint cream
2 oranges
1 dessertspoon butter
1 dessertspoon brown sugar
2 or more tots brandy
chopped walnuts for decoration

Slice the sponge into three layers.

To make the syrup, melt the butter with the brown sugar over a very low heat. Grate and squeeze the oranges and add the peel and juice to the melted butter and sugar. Simmer gently, then add the brandy. Allow to cool.

Whip and slightly sweeten the cream. Pour half the syrup over the bottom layer of sponge and then spread with a third of the cream. Arrange a third of the mandarin orange segments over the cream and place the middle layer of sponge on top. Repeat the procedure.

Use the remaining cream and mandarin oranges to decorate the top and sides of the cake. Chopped walnuts around the sides give the cake a finished look and add to the flavour.

Ivy Bush Royal Hotel
Carmarthen, Dyfed

Managing Director S A Kaminski
Chef M R du Mayne

Leek and potato mutton broth

1 lb leeks
8 oz potatoes
1 oz butter
1½ pints white stock
mutton trimmings
salt, pepper

Cut the white and light green parts of the leeks into ¼ inch squares. Slowly cook in the butter in a covered pan until soft but not coloured. Add the trimmings of mutton. Add the stock and the potatoes cut into ¼ inch cubes. Season to taste.

Simmer until the leeks and potatoes are cooked, approximately 15 minutes.

Surprise eggs

4 baked potatoes
4 eggs
1 oz butter
1 oz grated Parmesan cheese
salt, cayenne pepper
parsley to garnish

Cut a thin slice lengthwise off each hot baked potato. Scoop out the centre and pour one raw egg into each potato case.

Melt the butter and add the mashed potato removed from the jackets. Add seasoning and pile the mixture around the eggs in the cases.

Bake in a hot oven (Gas Mark 8, 450°F) for 10 minutes.

Sprinkle with the cheese and brown under the grill. Garnish with parsley, place on a hot dish and serve at once.

Ivy Bush Royal Hotel

Risotto casimir

1 lb veal
3 oz butter
3 oz flour
1 small onion
3 oz curry powder
½ glass white wine
¼ pint cream
2 bananas
4 pineapple rings
1 tablespoon pineapple juice
4 cherries
¾ pint chicken stock
oil

Melt the butter in a saucepan, add the chopped onion and sauté until lightly cooked. Add flour and curry powder. Stir in the pineapple juice, stock, cream and wine.

Simmer for 20 minutes.

Season to taste and pass through a fine strainer.

Cook the veal in a sauté pan, on a very fast heat, in a small amount of oil.

Poach the sliced banana and pineapple rings.

Add the meat to the sauce and place in a serving dish. Place the hot banana and pineapple rings on the sauce and meat. Place a cherry in each pineapple ring.

Braised Welsh calves livers with a marinated raisin sauce

2 lb Welsh calves livers
10 oz raisins marinated in red wine until blown out
4 oz chopped shallots
¼ pint red wine
1 oz butter
2 oz clarified margarine
1 tablespoon vinegar
flour
salt, pepper
1 onion and bacon slices for garnish

for the demi-glace sauce:
1¼ pint beef stock
1 oz flour
1 oz butter
1 medium sized onion
2 large mushrooms
2 tomatoes
1 rasher bacon
bouquet garni
2 tablespoons sherry

Heat an aluminium frying pan coated with the clarified margarine. Cut the liver into ¼ inch thick slices. Season, lightly flour and place into the just smoking-temperature pan.

Cook as desired, (rare, medium etc.).

Add the chopped shallots. Swill with the vinegar, then add the raisins. Shake the pan and add the red wine. Allow to reduce by two-thirds. Add the demi-glaze sauce and re-boil.

To make the demi-glace sauce, using a separate pan, chop the onion, mushrooms, tomatoes and bacon and fry in the butter for 5 minutes, stirring continuously. Blend in the flour and cook for a further 5 minutes. Gradually stir in the beef stock and add the herbs. Bring to the boil and simmer for 40 minutes. Sieve the sauce. Season and add the sherry.

Decanter the liver slices onto a serving dish. Add 1 oz butter to the sauce and pour over the liver.

Garnish with fried onion and grilled bacon slices.

**Gwesty Plas Glansevin
Plas Glansevin Hotel
Llangadog, Dyfed**

Proprietors William and Gwenda Rees
Chef Gwenda Rees

Melon salad with hot herb bread

½ melon
¼ cucumber
2 large tomatoes
salt

for the dressing:
1 tablespoon wine vinegar
pinch of salt
pinch of pepper
pinch of sugar
2 tablespoons salad oil
1 teaspoon chopped chives
1 teaspoon chopped parsley

for the herb bread:
1 French loaf or 2 small Vienna rolls
4 oz butter
a little lemon juice
1 clove garlic, crushed
dried mixed herbs

Peel and cube the cucumber, sprinkle with salt, cover and allow to stand
for 30 minutes. Peel and cube the melon and tomatoes, discarding the
pips.

To make the dressing, add the salt, pepper and sugar to the wine
vinegar and whisk in the oil a little at a time.

Wash and drain the cucumber and add to the melon and tomatoes.
Pour the dressing over the salad and chill for several hours. Before
serving, add the parsley and chives.

To make the herb bread, cream together the butter, lemon juice, garlic and mixed herbs. Cut the loaf into fairly thick slices and spread with the herb butter. Re-assemble the loaf. Spread the remaining butter over the crust. Wrap in foil and place in a hot oven (Gas Mark 7, 425°F) for about 10 minutes. Open the foil and allow a few minutes more in the oven for the crust to crispen.

Serve immediately with the melon salad.

Apple pudding

1 lb cooking apples
brown sugar
2 oz margarine
2 oz flour
¾ pint milk
2 oz sugar
2 drops vanilla essence
2 eggs, separated

Peel, core and slice the apples and arrange in a pudding basin. Sprinkle with brown sugar.

Melt the margarine and add the flour making a roux. Remove from the heat and add the milk. Bring to the boil, stirring continuously. Add the sugar and the vanilla essence. Leave to cool. Beat the two egg yolks and add to the cooled mixture. Whisk the egg whites and fold into the mixture. Place this mixture on top of the apples. Bake in a moderate oven (Gas Mark 4, 350°F) until golden and risen.

Like many of the dishes served at Glansevin, this is based on a traditional Welsh recipe.

Gwesty Plas Glansevin
Plas Glansevin Hotel

Bread and butter pudding with pears

6 slices well buttered bread
2 ripe pears
3 eggs
1 pint creamy milk
1 oz sugar (according to taste)
cinnamon

Cut three slices of the buttered bread into fingers and arrange in a pudding basin or soufflé dish. Peel and core the pears and place the four halves on the bread and butter fingers. Cover the pears with the remaining bread and butter cut into fingers, keeping the buttered sides uppermost.

Beat the eggs, add the scalded milk, sugar and a little cinnamon. Strain and pour over the bread and butter and pears. Sprinkle with cinnamon and place the basin in a roasting tin half full of water.

Cook in a moderate oven (Gas Mark 4, 350°F) for about 30 minutes, until set and the top evenly browned.

Pancakes in orange sauce

for the batter:
4 oz plain flour
pinch of salt
2 eggs
½ pint milk
1 tablespoon oil or melted butter

for the sauce:
juice of 2 oranges
grated rind of 1 orange
4 oz butter
4 oz sugar

castor sugar

To make the batter, sift the flour and salt together into a basin. Make a well in the centre and add the eggs. Add the milk a little at a time and beat thoroughly. Leave to stand for at least 30 minutes. Cook the pancakes in the oil or melted butter and put aside on a wire tray.

To make the orange sauce, place the ingredients in a frying pan and melt. Simmer gently until the sauce begins to thicken and becomes syrupy.

Place the pancakes in the sauce and fold into quarters. Simmer in the sauce for a few minutes until thoroughly saturated.

Lift the pancakes from the pan and place on a warm serving plate. Dredge with castor sugar and serve very hot.

Although pancakes are very popular in Wales as a tea time treat, they are rarely served as a dessert on a dinner menu. This is only one suggestion, the variations are endless.

The Cawdor Arms Hotel
Llandeilo, Dyfed

Catering Manager Peter Grey-Hughes

Norwegian prawns

1 lb large cooked prawns, fresh or frozen
    (Norwegian variety recommended)
4 tablespoons mayonnaise
4 thick slices fresh pineapple
1 pint fresh double cream
curry powder to taste
4 oz long grain rice

for garnish:

fresh lemon
tomato
cucumber
paprika
chopped parsley

Boil the rice and allow to cool. Allow the prawns to thaw naturally, drain well.

Whip the cream until really stiff. Place the mayonnaise in a bowl, add the whipped cream and bind together. Chop the pineapple into small chunks and add to the mixture. Add the prawns and mix well. Add curry powder to taste.

Place the mixture in individual glass bowls and arrange the rice around the edge. Decorate with wedges of lemon, tomato and cucumber. Sprinkle with paprika and chopped parsley.

Les escalopes de veau Marlborough

8 small escalopes veal

for the duxelle:

2 oz chopped mushrooms
2 oz chopped onions
2 oz chopped peppers
pinch of Tarragon
pinch of parsley
2 oz fresh breadcrumbs
2 oz butter
salt, pepper
oil

for the sauce:

2 measures Calvados
2 oz chopped pineapple
2 oz sliced mushrooms
2 oz chopped onions
2 oz sliced green peppers
¾ pint cream
salt, pepper

To make the duxelle, sweat the onions, peppers, Tarragon, mushrooms and parsley in the butter. Add breadcrumbs and season. Leave the mixture to cool.

Put the mixture on four escalopes of veal and place the other four on top of them, beat down around the edges. Fry gently in a little oil and when lightly browned add the onion, pineapple, mushrooms and peppers. Sauté quickly off. De-glaze the pan with Calvados, add the cream and reduce until the sauce thickens. Season.

Serve the veal and the sauce with pommes parisienne and stuffed tomatoes.

Heatherslade Bay Hotel
Southgate, near Swansea, West Glamorgan

Chocolate crumb cake

8 oz broken biscuits
3 oz margarine
1 tablespoon golden syrup
1 tablespoon sugar
1 tablespoon cocoa
2 oz block chocolate or chocolate drops

Crisp the biscuits thoroughly in a cool oven, then crumble finely.

Cream the margarine, syrup and sugar, warming the basin slightly. Stir the cocoa into the mixture, and then the crumbs.

Pack the mixture into a greased flan ring or sandwich tin lined with a round of greased paper.

Grate the block of chocolate and sprinkle on top of the cake, or cover the cake with the chocolate drops. Place the cake in a warm place to melt the chocolate slightly.

Remove from the flan ring or if a sandwich tin has been used, loosen the cake around the sides with a knife before taking it out of the tin, or it may crumble.

Plum compote with rich almond cake

for the plum compote:

1 lb red plums
1 glass red wine or port
4 tablespoons red-currant jelly
grated rind and juice of 1 orange

for the rich almond cake:

4 oz butter
5 oz castor sugar
3 eggs
3 oz ground almonds
1½ oz flour
2-3 drops almond essence

To make the rich almond cake, grease and flour a sandwich tin and cover the base with a disc of greaseproof paper. Set the oven at Gas Mark 4, 350°F. Soften the butter in a bowl using a wooden spoon. Add the sugar, a tablespoon at a time, and beat thoroughly until the mixture is soft and light. Add the eggs, one at a time, adding one-third of the ground almonds with each egg. Beat well. Fold in the flour and the almond essence using a metal spoon. Turn the cake mixture into the prepared tin.

Bake in the pre-heated oven for 45-50 minutes until the cake is cooked. (Test by inserting a thin skewer; it should come out clean. When cooked, the cake should also shrink very slightly from the sides of the tin.)

To make the plum compote, pour the wine into a large pan and boil until reduced by half. Add the red-currant jelly, stirring gently until dissolved, then add the orange rind and juice.

Halve and stone the plums and place in the pan with their cut sides uppermost. Allow the syrup to boil up and over the fruit, then poach gently until the fruit is quite tender. (Allow a full 10 minutes for this, even if the fruit is ripe.)

Place the compote in a bowl and allow to cool. Serve with the rich almond cake.

Osborne Hotel
Langland Bay, Swansea, West Glamorgan

Manager C J Smith

Roast duck Osborne

2 x 4 lb fresh ducks
salt, pepper
12 oz honey
1 lb whole chestnuts

Prepare the ducks with seasoning etc for roasting in an open roasting tray. Roast in the normal way in a moderately hot oven (Gas Mark 5, 375°F) at 20 minutes per lb.

When roasted, remove the ducks from the roasting tray and drain off all excess fat. Place the ducks in a large casserole dish. Place the honey and chestnuts over the ducks. Place the lid on the casserole and bake in the oven for another 10 minutes.

Serve half a duck per portion with a sauce made by the reduction of the honey and chestnuts.

Dragon Hotel
Kingsway Circle, Swansea, West Glamorgan

Ris d'agneau Prince de Galles

1 lb lamb sweetbreads
3 whole chicken liver
2 oz butter
flour
salt, pepper
3 fl oz Madeira wine
3 fl oz cream

Cut the sweetbreads and chicken livers into 1 inch pieces and dip in flour.

Sauté in melted butter and season. While the pan is still hot, add the Madeira. Finish by pouring in the cream, mix and serve immediately.

The Drangway
66 Wind Street, Swansea, West Glamorgan

Proprietor Colin Pressdee

Turbot with mussel sauce

1 large turbot (over 7 lb)
court-bouillon for cooking the fish (generally consists of water, salt,
    peppercorns, sliced onion, lemon juice and bouquet garni)
butter
flour
1 pint clean small mussels in their shells
cream
cinnamon
parsley for garnish

Trim the turbot and cut into 12 oz steaks. Reserve the trimmings.

To make fish stock, simmer the fish trimmings in salted water for about
30 minutes. (Add onion, celery, bay leaf etc if required.)

To make a light fish velouté sauce, mix equal quantities of butter and
flour to form a roux. Gradually add the fish stock to the roux, bring to
the boil, stirring continuously and simmer.

Gently poach the turbot steaks in the well seasoned court-bouillon until
cooked. Remove the fish from the liquid, remove the skin and arrange
the fish steaks on a serving dish.

Meanwhile in a small pan, heat the velouté sauce and add the mussels.
Cook quickly until all the shells are well open. Add cream and a little
cinnamon.

To serve, pour the mussel sauce over the turbot steaks and top
generously with finely chopped parsley. Serve immediately.

Welsh chicken

1 chicken, cut into quarters
4 oz Welsh bacon, diced
1 medium sized onion, diced
2 carrots, sliced
1 leek, sliced (reserving the white)
oil and butter for frying
sweet basil
salt, pepper
grated Caerphilly cheese
light chicken velouté sauce (Make a roux by blending butter and flour,
    add chicken stock, bring to the boil and simmer.)

Fry the bacon in oil and butter until crisp. Remove from the pan. Cook
the onion in the pan until transparent, then remove. Brown the chicken
pieces in the flavoured oil in the pan.

Add the onion, carrots, leek, herbs and seasoning and continue to cook
until the vegetables are lightly browned. Add the light chicken velouté
sauce and cook for about 10 minutes until the chicken is cooked
through.

Arrange the chicken and vegetables in a pre-heated earthenware dish
and cover with the grated cheese and bacon pieces. Brown in the oven
or under the grill. Serve immediately.

Fillet steak Cleopatra

4 x 8 oz fillet steaks
4 oz soft herring roes
4 oz asparagus
8 oz smoked bacon
4 eggs
butter for grilling
salt, pepper
4 large croûtons

for the sauce:
2 teaspoons French mustard
2 tablespoons brandy
double cream

Make a pouch in each steak and place the herring roes inside. Place bacon around the outside of each steak and hold in position with cocktail sticks. Brush with butter and grill. Season with salt and pepper.

Place cooked asparagus on top, then top this with a poached egg. Serve on croûtons accompanied by the sauce.

To make the sauce, add the mustard to a little double cream, heat gently and stir in the brandy.

Suprême of chicken Porthcawl

2 whole chickens (with the legs removed)
 or 4 suprêmes
4 oz butter
8 oz white mushrooms
6 oz chicken liver pâté
2 glasses white wine
2 medium-sized onions
½ pint fresh double cream (single cream can be
  used, but results are not as good)
salt, pepper
chopped parsley for garnish

Remove the small fillet at the back of the suprême, (the one with the sinew running down), and flatten gently. Cut a small slit in the side of each suprême (bone side), to form a pocket (about 1½ inches long).

Divide the pâté into 4 equal portions and insert into the pockets made in the suprêmes. Cover the pâté with the flattened fillets, tucking them into the suprêmes. Bring over the sides of the suprême to completely hide the stuffing operation. Season the suprêmes.

Melt the butter in a pan and heat gently. Gently cook the finely chopped onions in the butter for 2 minutes. Add the suprêmes and cook for 5 minutes. Turn the suprêmes over to cook on the other side, being careful not to colour too much. Add the sliced mushrooms and cook for a further 10 minutes, then add the white wine and bring to the boil. Add the cream and bring to the boil. Season the sauce to taste.

Remove the suprêmes and place on a serving dish. Cover with the sauce. Sprinkle with chopped parsley and serve immediately.

Quaintways Restaurant
Llantwit Major, South Glamorgan

Proprietor/Chef David Edward Jones

Pork tenderloin with prunes

2 pork tenderloin fillets (choose two fat-free fillets of equal
    size cut from underside of loin, about 2 lb)
18 large prunes
tea
6 anchovy fillets
milk
6 almonds, blanched
1½ oz butter
1 dessertspoon flour
½ pint jellied stock
salt, pepper
2 glasses red wine
12 pickling onions
1 teaspoon arrowroot (if necessary)

Soak the prunes overnight in freshly brewed tea. Stone the prunes just before using. Soak the anchovy fillets in milk for 30 minutes.

Make a slit down the length of each pork fillet and open it gently. Stuff six of the prunes with an anchovy fillet wrapped around a blanched almond. Lay the stuffed prunes along the opening of one of the fillets. Cover this fillet by laying the second opened-out fillet on top. Tie the fillets firmly together with string.

Brown the tied fillets on all sides in the butter in a shallow pan. Dust with the flour and cook for 2-3 minutes.

Meanwhile, cook the remaining prunes by simmering in the wine until tender and most of the wine has evaporated. Boil the onions in salted water until tender. Drain and keep hot.

To serve, carve the meat in slices (removing the string) and arrange on a hot serving dish. Tip the wine from the prunes into the sauce from the pork fillets and bring to the boil. (If necessary, thicken with arrowroot mixed with 1 tablespoon stock or water.) Adjust the seasoning and spoon the sauce over the meat.

Garnish with the soaked prunes and onions, mixed together.

Recommended wine: White wine (Loire)

Jamaican baked bananas

6 bananas
1 fresh coconut
¾ pint boiling water
1-2 tablespoons rum
2 tablespoons soft brown sugar

Grate the coconut flesh using the coarse side of the grater. Pour the boiling water over the grated coconut, cover and infuse for 30 minutes. Strain the infused coconut through a piece of muslin and squeeze well to extract the milk.

Slice the bananas straight into an oven-proof dish. Sprinkle with the rum and cover with the coconut milk. Dust the top with the brown sugar. Bake in a pre-heated moderately hot oven (Gas Mark 5, 375°F) for 30 minutes.

This dish is prepared with fresh coconut milk in Jamaica. In Britain coconut milk can be made by infusing freshly grated coconut.

The City Inn
City, Llansannor, near Cowbridge, South Glamorgan

Proprietor Mrs M Arbourne

Marrow Provençale

1 marrow (or 1 lb courgettes)
2 onions
½ lb butter
1 lb tomatoes
1 clove garlic
salt, pepper

Peel, de-pip and dice the marrow into 1 inch cubes. Roughly cut the onions. Blanch the tomatoes in boiling water for 10 seconds and chop them after removing the skins.

Melt the butter in a saucepan, add the onions and sweat off for 5 minutes with the lid on the saucepan. Add the marrow, tomatoes, crushed garlic, salt and pepper. Cook until the marrow is tender.

The Bear Hotel
Cowbridge, South Glamorgan

Braised ox-tail

4 lb ox-tail
6 oz celery
6 oz carrots
4 medium sized onions
½ pint red wine
2 tablespoons tomato purée
2 bay leaves
2½ pints demi-glace sauce
thyme
rosemary
juniper berries
salt, pepper

Divide the ox-tail at the joints. Roast the pieces of tail in a pan for 10-15 minutes and then place in a moderate oven (Gas Mak 4, 350°F) for 1 hour.

Cut the carrots into thin round slices, slice the celery crosswise and roughly chop the onions.

Remove the ox-tail from the pan. Place the carrots, celery and onions in the pan, braise and colour. Stir in the tomato purée. Add the wine, herbs and demi-glace.

Replace the ox-tail in the pan. Cover with foil and braise in a moderate oven for 3 hours.

Caso Paco Restaurant
Barry, South Glamorgan

Stuffed peppers

4 large peppers
¼ lb boiled rice
chopped parsley
1 clove garlic
1 egg
2 tablespoons oil
½ lb sausage meat
½ lb minced pork
a little stock
breadcrumbs
butter
salt, pepper
½ pint tomato sauce (see next recipe)

Mix the rice with the chopped parsley, crushed garlic, the egg, salt and pepper and 1 tablespoon of oil. Mix in the sausage meat and minced pork.

Cut the tops off the peppers and remove the seeds. Wash out well and place in a saucepan of salted boiling water. Allow to simmer gently for about 10 minutes.

Remove and dry the peppers. Stuff the peppers with the mixture. Place upright on an oiled meat tin, add a little stock and sprinkle the tops with breadcrumbs and a little butter. Cook slowly in a moderate oven (Gas Mark 4, 350°F) for 1 hour.

Remove from the oven and cover with tomato sauce (see next recipe). Replace in the oven for a further 30 minutes.

Tomato sauce

ingredients for 2 pints
¼ lb onions
¾ lb carrots
¾ lb celery
2 oz bacon trimmings
1 bay leaf
sprig of thyme
2 oz flour
½ pint tomato purée
2 pints brown stock
pinch of sugar
butter
salt, pepper

Dice the onions, carrots, celery and bacon. Sauté in a little butter with the bay leaf and thyme. Add the flour and cook over a low heat for 5 minutes, stirring constantly. Add the tomato purée and stir well. Add the stock. Cover and cook in a slow oven (Gas Mark 2, 300°F) for 1 hour.

Strain the sauce and season lightly. Add a pinch of sugar and 2 oz of butter.

This tomato sauce can be used as an accompaniment to a great number of dishes. It is also used as an ingredient in many recipes and is ideal for use with stuffed peppers.

Four Lanterns Restaurant
Barry, South Glamorgan

Proprietor Dimitri Johnson
Chef Katerina Johnson

Afelia with Cyprus style fried potatoes

4 thick slices gammon (or 4 pork cutlets)
4 glasses dry red wine
4 heaped teaspoons crushed coriander seeds
1 lb potatoes
vegetable oil for frying

Soak the meat in the wine and half of the coriander seeds for about 24 hours.

Peel the potatoes and cut into thick slices (thicker than for fritters). Deep fry in oil.

Remove the meat from the wine and fry in oil for a few minutes on each side. (If using pork, season with salt and cook for a little longer than gammon.) To the fried meat, add the wine from the marinade, the remaining two teaspoons of coriander seeds and the fried potatoes. Cover and simmer gently for about 30 minutes. Shake the pan occasionally to let the meat and potato absorb the wine.

Serve with fresh salad.

Dolmades

8 oz packet or tin of vine leaves
1 lb minced meat
1 onion, finely chopped
2 teaspoons chopped mint
1 teaspoon cinnamon
6 tablespoons tomato purée
3 cloves garlic, finely chopped
12 oz rice
juice of 2 lemons
oil
salt, black pepper

Fry the onion in oil until transparent. Add the minced meat and fry for 10-15 minutes over a low heat. Add the mint, cinnamon, 3 tablespoons of tomato purée, garlic, rice, salt and pepper. Remove from the heat and leave to cool for 15 minutes.

Wash the vine leaves and separate them. Using a teaspoon, place a small amount of the mixture in the centre of each vine leaf. Fold and roll the leaf to give a "dolma".

In a saucepan put ½ pint of water, 5 oz of oil and 3 tablespoons of tomato purée. Bring to the boil. Find two heavy plates the same size as the base of the saucepan. Place one plate upside-down in the saucepan. Carefully place the dolmades, one by one, tightly together on the plate in the saucepan. Squeeze the lemon juice over the dolmades, cover with boiling water and add a little salt. Place the second plate upside-down over the dolmades to hold them in position. (It is important that the top plate is heavy and stays in position, so that the dolmades do not open whilst boiling.) Boil slowly for 60-90 minutes.

Serve with fresh salad.

Boiled cabbage leaves or other vegetables may be used instead of vine leaves as variations on this recipe.

Sully House Restaurant
Swanbridge, South Glamorgan

Proprietor G R Collis

Crêpes aux fruits de mer

8 small unsweetened pancakes
12 oz assorted fish (prawns, scallops, scampi, Dover sole etc.)
flour
salt, pepper
6 mushrooms
butter
½ onion
½ pint fish stock
2 tablespoons double cream
4 oz grated strong cheese
2 small knobs beurre-manié (made by mixing equal quantities
 of softened butter and flour to form a paste)
2 tablespoons fish sauce (made by adding fish stock to a roux
   made from equal quantities of margarine and flour)

Cook the pancakes, fold them in half, place on serving dish and keep warm.

Season the fish and cut into small pieces (approximately 1 inch). Dust in flour. Fry quickly in hot butter. Add the sliced mushrooms and finely chopped onion and mix well. Add the stock, fish sauce and cream and simmer gently for a few minutes.

Remove the fish from the sauce and arrange over the pancakes. Stir the beurre-manié into the sauce to thicken it. Add the cheese and mix well.

Cover the fish with the sauce and place under the grill to brown. Serve immediately.

Recommended wine: Puligny Montrachet H. Boillot, D.B.

Carré d'agneau en croûte

1 x 4 lb saddle of lamb
4 rashers bacon
2 oz finely chopped onion
2 oz finely chopped mushrooms
¼ pint brown sauce
¾ lb puff pastry
salt, pepper

Bone the saddle of lamb and trim off excess fat. Season and fry quickly in a frying pan. Remove the lamb and fry the bacon in the pan. Remove the bacon and fry the chopped onion and mushrooms. Add the brown sauce to the onion and mushrooms.

Place the lamb on a wire rack. Cover with the onion and mushroom mixture and the bacon. Allow to cool.

Roll out the puff pastry thinly. Wrap the pastry around the lamb, sealing the edges. Bake in a moderately hot oven (Gas Mark 5, 375°F).

To serve, cut into slices approximately 1 inch thick.

Recommended wine: Chateau St. Pierre Sevaistre St. Julian C.B. (Claret) or Volnay, Jos Drouchin F. B. (Red Burgundy)

Caprice Restaurant
The Esplanade, Penarth, South Glamorgan

Proprietor E Rabaiotti

Tagliatelle Alfredo

10 oz tagliatelle or noodles
6 oz shredded ham
2 oz butter
2 oz Parmesan cheese
2 oz finely chopped parsley
6 fl oz fresh double cream
1 small clove garlic, crushed
salt, pepper

Place the pasta in boiling salted water and cook until tender. Drain the pasta and keep hot.

Melt the butter in a saucepan and add the ham, garlic, Parmesan cheese, half of the chopped parsley and mix together. Add the cooked pasta and stir until well mixed. Add the cream and salt and pepper to taste. Continue to stir over heat until the mixture is well blended.

Place the mixture on a serving dish and sprinkle with the remaining chopped parsley. Serve immediately.

Vittello Pizziaola

1 lb veal escalopes or 4 veal cutlets
1 tablespoon olive oil, 1 oz butter
flour
2 oz stuffed olives
1 oz chopped capers
2 oz finely chopped onion
2 oz finely chopped anchovies
1 clove garlic, crushed
6 medium sized tomatoes, peeled, seeded and chopped
    or 1 small tin peeled tomatoes, drained and chopped

1 level teaspoon oregano
1 oz chopped parsley
2 fl oz fresh cream
salt, pepper

Flour and season the veal. Heat the oil and butter in a frying pan until it bubbles. Add the veal and cook for 2 minutes on each side. Remove from the pan and keep hot.

Place the olives, capers, onion, anchovies and garlic into the frying pan and cook slowly without colouring. Add the chopped tomatoes, oregano and parsley. Bring to the boil and cook for 2 minutes.

Place the veal in the pan and cook for a further 2 minutes, turning frequently. Remove the veal from the sauce and place on a serving dish. Add the cream to the sauce and bring to the boil. Pour the sauce over the veal and serve immediately.

Zabaglione Caprice

6 egg yolks
6 oz castor sugar
8 fl oz Marsala wine
1 fl oz rum
1 fl oz brandy
8 sponge fingers

To prepare this dish, a double-saucepan is needed. (A glass oven-proof bowl which fits inside a saucepan of boiling water can be used.)

Whisk the egg yolks and sugar, in the double-saucepan, until light and fluffy. Mix in the Marsala gradually. Place on the heat and whisk continuously until the mixture thickens.

Add the brandy and rum and serve immediately as the mixture collapses very quickly.

Serve with sponge fingers.

Glendale Hotel
Penarth, South Glamorgan

Proprietors A Nicholas and A Zanellato
Chef A Zanellato

Stracciatella soup

2 pints chicken stock
4 medium eggs
mixed herbs
salt, pepper
fresh parsley and Parmesan cheese for garnish

Bring the chicken stock to the boil. Season with mixed herbs, salt and pepper. Boil for 3 minutes.

Break the eggs into the stock, beating to break them up. Boil for a few minutes.

Serve the soup sprinkled with chopped parsley and grated Parmesan cheese.

Plymouth Arms
St Fagans, South Glamorgan

Tŷ potatoes

3 lb potatoes (choose good floury potatoes of equal size)
1 lb diced onion and tomato
4 oz butter
grated cheese
salt, pepper

Wash the potatoes and bake them in their jackets, on a baking tray, for
40 minutes. Allow to cool and cut in half. Scoop the potato out of the
skins. Add the diced onion and tomato and the butter to the potato.
Season with salt and pepper and mix together. Place the mixture back in
the shells. Sprinkle the top with grated cheese and bake in the oven for
10 minutes.

Welsh apple tart

18 oz shortcrust pastry
18 oz thick apple pieces
sugar
3 large apples
4 oz apricot jam
icing sugar

Stew the thick apple pieces with sugar until they are soft enough to form
a purée. Leave to cool.

Line a greased flan tin with the shortcrust pastry. Fill with the cold apple
purée and smooth the surface. Cut the three large apples into thin half-
moon slices. Cover the apple purée with these slices. Bake in a hot
oven, (Gas Mark 7, 425°F) for 25-30 minutes.

When baked, spread a layer of apricot jam on top of the apples and
sprinkle with icing sugar.

Harvesters
5 Pontcanna Street, Cardiff, South Glamorgan

Proprietors Mr and Mrs Giampiero Famá

Kedgeree

1 small onion
1 small capsicum (pepper) preferably red
1 teaspoon paprika
pinch of cayenne
4 oz cooked, flaked Finnan haddock
½ lb long grain rice, parboiled with salt and a teaspoon
   of tumeric
1 tablespoon double cream
salt, pepper
2 oz butter
1 hard boiled egg
parsley for garnish

Dice the onion and pepper and fry in the butter until soft. Add the
paprika, cayenne, haddock and salt and pepper to taste. Heat through
slowly, then add the rice and fry briskly until crisp. Mix in the double
cream and arrange on plates.

Garnish with chopped egg and parsley.

Kedgeree can be served as a spicy first course. For use as a main
course, increase the ingredients by 50% and serve with a tomato salad.

Recommended wine: chilled hock such as Rudesheimer Rosengarten.

Jugged hare

1 medium sized hare
1 lb onions
1 whole celery
1 bottle red wine
3 pints good stock
bouquet garni, made from herbs and garlic
8 fl oz port
Worcestershire sauce
red-currant jelly
1½ oz blue cheese
2 oz plain chocolate
1 lb button mushrooms
¼ lb stoneless olives
salt, pepper
vegetable oil
parsley for garnish

The hare should be hung for about a week or ten days according to taste, then skinned, cut in half lengthways and each half cut into four. (Your butcher may do this for you.)

Dice the onions and celery and place in a large non-metal container with the wine, stock and bouquet garni. Submerge the hare in this marinade and leave in a cool place to marinate for two days.

Remove the hare, place the marinade in a stew pan and bring to the boil. Fry the hare pieces lightly in oil and return them to the mixture. Add the port, Worcestershire sauce, red-currant jelly, blue cheese and chocolate, then the mushrooms and olives. Simmer for about an hour, until the meat begins to loosen on the bone of the foreleg portions.

Place in an earthenware dish and garnish generously with parsley.

Serve with new potatoes boiled in their jackets and a lightly cooked green vegetable.

Recommended wine: full bodied red burgundy

Gibson's Restaurant
8 Romilly Crescent, Cardiff, South Glamorgan

Proprietor/Chef Irene Canning

Artichoke soup

2 large globe artichokes (end of season artichokes
 which are woody or bruised may be used)
2 pints chicken stock
1 tablespoon vegetable oil
½ oz butter
2 egg yolks
4 fl oz double cream
salt, pepper
chopped parsley for garnish

Clean the artichokes under running water. Remove the bruised leaves.
Place the artichokes in a saucepan and add enough of the boiling stock
to cover them. Add the butter and oil and boil for about 40 minutes.

Remove the artichokes and drain. Dismantle the artichokes, discarding
everything except the hearts. Dice the hearts and add to the stock left in
the saucepan. Add the remaining stock. Bring to the boil. Taste for
seasoning (oversalting slightly at this stage).

To serve, lightly beat the egg yolks and place in the serving terrine. In a
separate saucepan, gently heat the cream. Pour the hot cream onto the
egg yolks in the terrine, stirring continuously. Stir in the boiling stock.
Sprinkle with chopped parsley.

Recommended wine: dry fino sherry (chilled)

Maggie Gibson's chicken pie

1½ lb chicken
1 lb carrots
12 oz onions
6 oz peas
1 bouquet garni
½ lb sliced mushrooms
shortcrust pastry (made with butter)
beaten egg

for the velouté sauce à la creme:
¾ pint chicken stock (made during the poaching of the chicken)
2 oz butter
1½ oz plain flour
½ oz cornflour
1 glass dry white wine
¼ pint cream
sea salt, black pepper

Place the chicken in a large saucepan and cover with cold water. Add the whole peeled carrots and onions and the bouquet garni. Bring to the boil and poach gently until the chicken is just cooked, (about 45 minutes). Remove the chicken and vegetables from the stock. Slice the carrots and onions and set aside. Remove the chicken from the bone and dice into large pieces.

Boil the stock until it has reduced to about ¾ pint. Whilst it is reducing, put the peas in the stock and remove when just cooked. Similarly, cook the mushrooms in the stock for a few minutes, remove and drain.

To make the sauce, melt the butter in a saucepan and add the flour and cornflour. Cook for about 5 minutes, stirring continuously, but do not allow to brown. Gradually add the wine and stock to make a smooth sauce. Cook gently for about 20 minutes, stirring occasionally. Add the cream and cook for a further few minutes. Season with sea salt and freshly ground black pepper.

Place the chicken and vegetables in a pie dish with a lip, cover with the sauce and allow to cool. Cover with shortcrust pastry. Brush the top with beaten egg.

Maggie Gibson's chicken pie

Bake in a moderately hot oven (Gas Mark 6, 400°F) for about 40 minutes.

Serve with plain fresh vegetables or follow with green salad.

Recommended wine: Beaujolais, Moselle or Chablis.

Brandy tulips

for the brandy snaps:
2 oz butter
2 oz sugar
2 oz golden syrup
2 oz flour
½ teaspoon ground ginger
juice of ¼ lemon

for decoration:
stem ginger slices

for filling:
orange segments
Grand Marnier
or
sliced white peaches
brandy

Melt the butter, sugar and syrup in a saucepan. Remove from the heat and add the warmed flour and the lemon juice and ginger. Stir well.

Cover a baking tray with non-stick paper. On this, place teaspoonfuls of the mixture about six inches apart, as the mixture spreads. Bake in a moderate oven, (Gas Mark 4, 350°F) for 10-15 minutes, until golden brown.

When cooked and still warm, remove each brandy snap with a palette knife. Mould each one into a small cup around the bottom of a buttered jam jar or small basin. If the mixture is too soft, allow to cool slightly — if too hard, return to the oven for a minute or two. These will keep for about a week in an airtight tin.

To serve, fill with either orange segments sprinkled with Grand Marnier or sliced white peaches with brandy. Decorate with stem ginger slices.

Savastano's Ristorante Italiano
302 North Road, Cardiff, South Glamorgan

Proprietor/Chef Giacomo Savastano

Spaghetti alla Carbonara

1 lb spaghetti
½ lb bacon
3 eggs
1 oz black pepper corns
salt
butter
grated Parmesan cheese for garnish

Add the spaghetti to boiling salted water and boil until cooked. Drain.

Brown the bacon in butter, add the black pepper and salt to taste. Add the spaghetti and cook for a few minutes. Beat the eggs and stir into the spaghetti. Cook for a few minutes more.

To serve, sprinkle with grated Parmesan cheese.

Flambé à la maître d'hôtel

2 measures Grand Marnier
knob of butter
8 peach halves
tin of Morella cherries
4 tablespoons castor sugar
brandy

Melt the castor sugar with the butter over a flame until runny.

Add the peaches and warm for about 2 minutes. Add the Grand Marnier, the black cherries and juice from the tin. Boil for 2½ minutes. Finally, flambé with the brandy.

La Locanda Restaurant
114 St. Mary Street, Cardiff

Manager Werner Fuchs

Fillet mignons à la Beaufremont

1 lb thinly sliced meat for frying (beef, veal or pork)
flour
egg
breadcrumbs
2 ½ oz butter
4 oz noodles or spaghetti

for the sauce:
¼ lb onions
2 cloves garlic
3 oz mushrooms
2 tomatoes
parsley
salt, pepper
1 oz butter
1 fl oz double cream
4 tablespoons white wine or dash of brandy
grated hard cheese for garnish

Coat the meat in flour, egg and breadcrumbs. Fry in 2 oz butter until golden brown. Remove from the pan and keep warm in the oven.

Boil the noodles or spaghetti. When cooked, strain and add ½ oz butter, salt and pepper. Arrange on a serving dish with the meat and keep warm in the oven.

To make the sauce, cook the chopped onions, crushed garlic and sliced mushrooms in 1 oz butter. Add chopped tomatoes and parsley and finally the cream and white wine or brandy. Season to taste. To add to the flavour, sprinkle with the grated cheese.

Positano Ristorante Italiano
9 Church Street, Cardiff, South Glamorgan

Saltimbocca alla Romana

16 slices veal
16 slices Parma ham
24 sage leaves
1 small glass dry white wine
butter for frying
flour
salt, pepper

Flatten the slices of veal and season with salt and pepper. Place the sage leaves (one or two according to size and taste) and a slice of ham on each slice of veal. Secure with a wooden cocktail stick and coat in flour.

Fry them fairly quickly in butter until brown. Remove the veal from the pan and place on a hot plate. De-glaze the pan with the wine, reduce slightly and pour over the veal.

The Spot Restaurant
7 Church Street, Cardiff, South Glamorgan

Proprietor David Evans
Chef Gernot Stoffaneller

Fillets of sole casimir

8 fillets of sole
¼ pint white wine
½ medium sized onion
1 oz parsley
juice of ½ lemon
1 pint curry sauce
tomato ketchup
3 tablespoons cream
clarified butter for frying
flour

for garnish:
pineapple cubes
sliced red peppers
roasted sliced almonds

Marinate the fillets of sole in the white wine, chopped onion, chopped parsley and lemon juice for about 2 hours.

Dip the fillets in flour and fry in clarified butter. Place the fried fillets on a serving dish and cover with the curry sauce (which should be slightly flavoured with tomato ketchup and cream).

Garnish with pineapple cubes, sliced red peppers and roasted sliced almonds.

Serve with pilaf rice.

Médaillons de veau Gourmet

1 ½ lb tenderloin of veal
1 shallot
1 measure Calvados brandy
clarified butter
¼ pint double cream
flour
4 oz mushrooms
3 medium-sized peeled tomatoes
¼ pint white stock
salt, pepper
Tabasco

Slice the veal into ½ inch slices, and flatten slightly. Season with salt and white pepper and dip in flour. Fry in clarified butter until golden brown.

Add the chopped shallot and finely chopped mushrooms and flame with Calvados brandy (apple brandy). Add the finely chopped tomatoes, stock and cream. Season with Tabasco, salt and pepper to taste and cook for 10 minutes.

Serve with rice.

Royal Hotel
St. Mary Street, Cardiff, South Glamorgan

General Manager Frank D Fuller

Paprika schnitzel

4 x 8 oz veal escalopes
salt
paprika
flour
butter

for the sauce:
1 green pepper
1 chopped onion
4 oz finely cut smoked bacon
1 clove garlic
1 oz paprika
brown sauce
1 lemon
fresh cream

Season the veal escalopes with salt and paprika. Flour them and cook in
a little butter.

To make the sauce, lightly sauté the chopped onion, green pepper,
bacon and garlic in a saucepan. Add the paprika, a little brown sauce,
the juice of the lemon and fresh cream. Boil for 2 minutes.

Angel Hotel
Castle Street, Cardiff, South Glamorgan

Manager Owen Jones

Cold avocado soup

4 over-ripe avocados
1 pint chicken stock (cold)
¼ pint single cream
½ level tablespoon curry powder

Remove the flesh from the avocados. Pass through a sieve or liquidize with a little of the stock. Mix all the ingredients. Whisk and place in the refrigerator.

Serve when well chilled.

Duck à l'orange

2 x 3lb ducks
¼ pint orange juice
4 oz sugar
1 pint unseasoned demi-glace sauce
4 oranges
2 tots Grand Marnier

Cook the ducks until tender and crisp, then remove legs and breasts.

Place the orange juice and sugar in a thick-bottomed pan. Cook until almost caramelized. Add the demi-glace and remove from the heat.

Scrape the outer edges of the oranges with a zesteur. Place the zest in a little water in a pan. Bring to the boil and remove the zest to use as decoration.

Segment the oranges and decorate a serving dish with both segments and zest. To serve, place the duck portions in the centre of this dish. Add the liqueur to the orange sauce and pour the sauce over the duck portions.

Roman Embassy Italian Restaurant
Senghenydd Road, Cardiff, South Glamorgan

Fillet steak Roman Embassy

4 fillet steaks
1 small onion
butter
salt, pepper
garlic
cream
brandy
parsley

for the Neopolitan sauce:

1 small onion
4 tomatoes or medium-sized tin
1 lb mushrooms
¼ pint stock
salt, pepper
olive oil
butter

To make the Neopolitan sauce, fry the finely chopped onion in the olive oil until golden brown. Fry the sliced mushrooms in butter and add to the cooked onion. Add the sieved or finely chopped tomatoes. Add the stock and let it boil gently for 1-2 hours until thickened. (If it tastes too sharp, a sprinkle of sugar may be added.)

Chop the onion finely and fry in butter until golden brown. Add a sprinkle of parsley and freshly ground pepper.

Flatten the steaks, rub with garlic and season with salt. Fry quickly in butter for about one minute on each side.

Add the Neopolitan sauce to the fried steaks and onion. Add a little brandy and a little single cream and stir over gentle heat. (Should you want to thicken the sauce further, it is best to use a sprinkle of arrowroot.)

Recommended wine: Amorone della Valpolicella, medium red wine or rosé.

Costa Brava Restaurant
117 Woodville Road, Cathays, Cardiff, South Glamorgan

Entrecôte Apollo

4 x 8 oz steaks
salt, pepper
butter
oil
grated cheese for garnish

for the sauce:
½ lb mushrooms
¼ lb shallots
1 dessertspoon French mustard
1 measure brandy
¼ pint demi-glace sauce
butter
salt, pepper

Trim any fat off the steaks and season with salt and pepper.

To make the sauce, slice the mushrooms and shallots, and fry gently in butter, seasoning well. Mix the mustard and the brandy and stir into the demi-glace sauce. Mix the shallots and mushrooms into the sauce and bring gently to the boil.

Fry the steaks in a mixture of butter and oil until cooked to taste.

Arrange the steaks on a serving dish, pour the sauce over them and garnish with grated cheese. Grill lightly for a few seconds until the cheese starts to melt. Serve with asparagus tips.

Suggested vegetables: braised celery, sautéed potatoes and French beans fried in butter.

Recommended wine: 1969 Nuits-Saint-Georges Patriache

Cyw iâr Eryri
Chicken Snowdonia

½ spring chicken per person
oil
French mustard
salt, pepper
chopped parsley for garnish

for the sauce:
½ pint stock
2 tablespoons cream
1 tablespoon brandy
¼ lb mushrooms
1 green pepper
Tabasco
salt, pepper

Sprinkle chicken with salt and pepper and spread with French mustard.
Fry chicken pieces slowly in oil, (at least ½ inch deep) until cooked
through and golden, about 20 minutes in a covered pan.

To make the sauce, steam or boil the chopped mushrooms and pepper.
Heat the stock in a separate pan, add the brandy and reduce. Add the
cream, mushrooms, pepper, dash of Tabasco, salt and pepper. Cook
gently for 5 minutes.

Serve over the chicken. Sprinkle with fresh chopped parsley.

Golwythau cig llo Tywysog Cymru
Cutlets of veal Prince of Wales

4 cutlets veal
4 slices mild cheese
flour
1 egg
breadcrumbs
2 oz butter
chopped parsley

for the sauce:
¼ pint cream
⅛ pint white wine
2 oz mushrooms

Remove bone from the veal. Coat in flour and dip in beaten egg and breadcrumbs. Fry for 5 minutes in the butter.

Cover each cutlet with a slice of cheese and grill until the cheese melts.

To make the sauce, boil the wine steadily until reduced. Stir in the cream and sliced mushrooms and cook until it thickens.

Serve over the cutlets. Sprinkle with fresh chopped parsley.

Lanterns Restaurant
41 Whitchurch Road, Cardiff, South Glamorgan

Prawn alagratin

1 lb cooked prawns
grated Parmesan cheese for garnish

for the cheese sauce:
4 oz grated Cheddar cheese
½ pint milk
1 oz flour
2 tablespoons cream
salt, pepper

Put the prawns into four terrines and place in the oven for 1-2 minutes to warm.

To make the cheese sauce, place the flour with the seasoning in a basin and gradually add a little of the milk, stirring to form a smooth paste. Boil the remainder of the milk and pour over the flour mixture, stirring all the time. Bring the sauce to the boil over a low heat, stirring until it thickens, and then add the cheese and cream.

Cover the prawns with the sauce. Place the terrines under the grill for about a minute.

Before serving, sprinkle with grated Parmesan cheese.

Post House Hotel
Pentwyn, Cardiff, South Glamorgan

Chef David Foster

Chicken Cardigan

4 chicken breasts
4 oz crabmeat
flour
salt, pepper
2 oz butter for frying
4 turned mushrooms
2 tablespoons sherry
4 fl oz tinned lobster bisque
2 fl oz cream
8 fl oz chicken velouté
chopped parsley for garnish

Remove the small fillet at the back of each chicken breast and flatten the fillet. Cut a slit in each breast to form a pocket. Place 1 oz of crabmeat in each pocket. Cover this with the flattened fillet and tuck it into the cavity.

Dust the chicken portions with seasoned flour and fry in the butter until golden brown, approximately 5 minutes.

Add the mushrooms, swill with the sherry and reduce by half. Add the chicken velouté, bisque and cream. Check the seasoning. Add lemon juice if required. Garnish with chopped parsley.

Six Bells Inn
Peterstone Wentlooge, South Glamorgan

Chef Peter Mario Saito

Avocado with sea food

2 avocado pears
2 peeled prawn tails
2 oz diced lobster
3 diced scampi
4 cleaved oysters
2 diced mushrooms
1 hard boiled egg
¼ pint mayonnaise
1 tablespoon grated horseradish
½ teaspoon mustard
1 tablespoon ketchup
1 tablespoon dry sherry
2 tablespoons unsweetened whipped cream
lemon juice
olive oil
salt, pepper
lettuce leaves and lemon for garnish

Halve the avocado pears lengthways. Remove the stones and scoop out the centres leaving ¼ inch of flesh.

Mix the lobster, prawns, scampi and raw mushrooms with the scooped out avocado flesh. Cover with lemon juice, olive oil, salt and pepper and allow to marinate in a cool place.

Mix the mayonnaise with the mustard, ketchup and sherry and season to taste. Fold in the whipped cream. Bind the salpicon of sea food with this sauce.

Fill the avocado halves with the mixture and sprinkle with chopped hard boiled egg. Place an oyster lightly coated with aspic on top. Serve well chilled on lettuce leaves and garnish with lemon.

Fillet de bœuf sauté strogonoff

1 ¼ lb tail fillet of beef
salt, pepper
2 large onions
¼ pint sour cream
a little red wine
1 teaspoon mustard
juice of ½ lemon
peppercorns
3 oz butter
¼ pint demi-glace sauce
chopped parsley for garnish

Remove the skin and fat from the meat and cut into thin slices.

Chop the onions and simmer in a little butter. Add the demi-glace and continue to cook.

Season the meat. Heat a little butter in a separate pan and quickly brown the meat on both sides (3-5 minutes). Place the meat on a sieve to drip.

Add sour cream to the meat juices left in the pan and reduce. Add the demi-glace with onion and bring to the boil. Remove from heat and season with the mustard, crushed peppercorns, lemon juice and red wine. Add the blood which has collected from the meat. Toss the meat into the sauce, but do not re-boil.

Serve on a bed of cooked rice, and garnish with parsley.

Six Bells Inn

Melon dessert

2 ripe melons
4 small scoops ice cream
sweet sherry
whipped cream, cherries and almonds for decoration

Cut the melons in half. Remove seeds and, using a round spoon, scoop out the flesh into small balls. Place a small scoop of ice cream into the bottom of each melon half. Place the melon balls on top. Add sweet sherry.

Decorate with whipped cream, cherries and almonds. Serve well chilled.

Conca d'Oro Restaurant
Newport, Gwent

Pâté Conca d'Oro

1 lb pork liver
½ lb pork fat
½ lb chicken liver
1 lb veal
6 egg whites
3 shallots
2 bay leaves
salt, freshly ground pepper

Strip and trim the pork liver and skin and trim the veal. Finely mince the chicken and pork liver and the veal, and then pass through a fine sieve.

Render the pork fat and infuse with the flavour of the finely chopped shallots and bay leaves. Using an electric mixer, mix this fat with the minced liver and veal, egg whites and seasoning.

Place the pâté in a terrine and place in a shallow pan containing boiling water. Cook for 2 hours in a slow oven (Gas Mark 2, 300°F). Leave to cool before serving.

(When the pâté is placed in the terrine the top can be sealed with melted butter.)

Pineapple Mexican

1 fresh ripe pineapple 1 ½-2 lbs in weight
coffee flavoured genoise sponge for base (about 8 oz cooked weight)
family block of dairy vanilla ice-cream
3 measures Tia Maria
1 pint whipped cream
glacé cherries and angelica for decoration

Cut the top and bottom off the pineapple. Retain the top. Slice around the inside of the skin with a sharp knife and remove the flesh of the fruit in one piece. Keep the shell. Slice the pineapple, (8 thin slices or 4 thick ones) and remove the hard core.

Soak the slices in the Tia Maria for about half an hour. (At this stage also you can sweeten with sugar to taste.)

Place a 4 inch wide strip of sponge on a serving dish and place ice-cream on top. Arrange the slices of pineapple on this and pipe the whipped cream to completely cover; decorate as you wish. Leave sufficient room to put the shell of the fruit at one end or at the side of the dish.

Cut diamond-shaped holes in the side of the pineapple shell, 6 or 8 should be sufficient. Take a night light or 1 inch piece of candle and light it. Place it in the space you left on the dish and put the shell over it. Put the top on. This will stay alight for about 10-15 minutes.

Three Blackbirds
Llantarnam, near Newport, Gwent

Manager Giovanni Delgrano

Petti di pollo alla Doney

4 breasts chicken
½ pint fresh cream
2 fl oz sweet sherry
2 fl oz brandy
French mustard
Senape (Italian mustard)
4 oz cooked mushrooms
2 oz onion
3 oz butter
2 oz plain flour
salt, pepper

Place the butter, chopped onion and floured breasts of chicken in a frying pan and cook the chicken for 7 minutes on each side. Spread the mustard over the chicken and season with salt and pepper. Add the sherry and brandy to the chicken in the pan and flambé. Cook for a further 5 minutes turning the chicken frequently. Add the mushrooms and the fresh cream. Simmer gently until the cream thickens. Serve immediately.

Suggested vegetables: Sautéed potatoes, garden peas, asparagus tips.

Beaufort Arms Hotel
Monmouth, Gwent

Nelson's casserole

8 oz prawns
8 oz scallops
8 oz mussels
8 oz scampi
4 tablespoons white wine
½ pint cream
butter
parsley for garnish

Sauté the prawns, scallops, mussels and scampi in a little butter. When cooked, add the white wine. Reduce slightly and then add the cream. Reduce to a thick consistency. Pour into a serving dish and garnish with parsley.

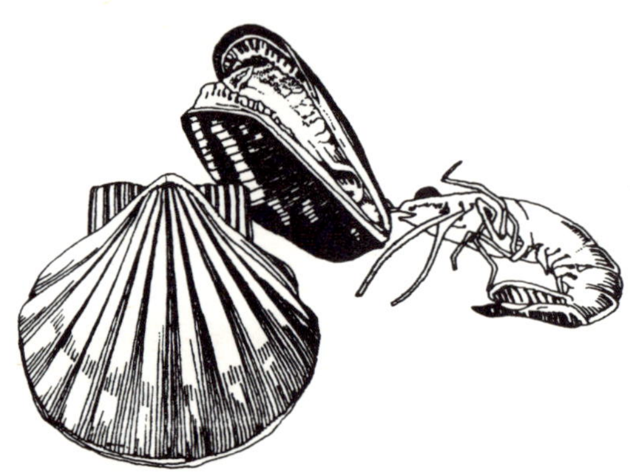

Tournedos Beaufort

4 x 8 oz fillet steaks
1 oz chopped onion
1 oz sliced mushrooms
2 oz pâté
2 tablespoons brandy
4 tablespoons white wine
4 slices bread
oil
cream
parsley or cress for garnish

Fry the steaks in a little oil. Remove from the pan and fry the onion, mushrooms and pâté. When the onion and mushrooms are cooked, add the brandy and flame. Add the white wine and then the cream.

Remove the crust from the bread and fry the slices of bread on both sides in a little oil.

Place the fried bread on a serving dish, place the steaks on top and pour the boiling sauce over them. Garnish with parsley or cress.

The Old Farmhouse Hotel
Llandogo, near Tintern, Gwent

Proprietor J C Northcroft
Chef A H Lewin

Old Farmhouse chicken liver pâté

¾ lb chicken livers
1 onion
2 oz English or Welsh butter
1 level teaspoon finely chopped parsley
1 standard egg
1 level teaspoon thyme
¼ teaspoon nutmeg
1 dessertspoon sherry or brandy
1 oz pork dripping
salt
freshly milled black pepper

Lightly fry the liver and chopped onion in the pork dripping until coloured. Mince the liver and onion finely, then pound with the butter until smooth and creamy. Blend in the beaten egg, parsley, thyme, nutmeg and the sherry or brandy. Season to taste with salt and pepper

Turn the mixture into a small earthenware dish and cook in a bain-marie in a moderate oven (Gas Mark 4, 350°F) for 30 minutes. Allow to cool, then chill for 2-3 hours.

Spoon portions of the pâté onto plates and serve with crisp fresh white toast cut into strips, with the crusts removed.

Index of hotels and restaurants

Alfredo Restaurant/Conwy	48
Angel Hotel/Cardiff	171
Bear Hotel/Cowbridge	149
Beaufort Arms/Monmouth	184
Beaufort Arms/Raglan	18
Blue Bell Inn/Llangurig	24
Bontddu Hall Hotel/Dolgellau	84
Bronheulog Hotel/Abersoch	71
Bryn Derwen Hotel/Llanbedrog	72
Bryn Morfydd Hotel/Denbigh	42
Buckingham Hotel/Tenby	123
Bulkeley Arms/Beaumaris	60
Caprice Restaurant/Penarth	156
Cartref Restaurant/St David's	107
Casa Paco Restaurant/Barry	150
Castle Hotel/Bangor	55
Cawdor Arms/Llandeilo	136
Cedars Hotel/Chepstow	16
Chequers/Northophall Village	39
Chez Gilbert/Haverfordwest	120
City Inn/Cowbridge	148
Cliff Hotel/Gwbert-on-sea	96
Coach House Inn/Pembroke	121
Conca d'Oro Restaurant/Newport	181
Conrah Hotel/Aberystwyth	92
Costa Brava Restaurant/Cardiff	173
Cripple Creek Inn/Raglan	17
Cuffern Hotel/Roch	116
Dive Inn/Tudweiliog	67
Dragon Hotel/Swansea	141
Drangway Hotel/Swansea	142
Druidstone Hotel/Druidston Haven	118
Eagles Hotel/Penmachno	54
Emlyn Arms/Newcastle Emlyn	94
Empire Hotel/Llandudno	46
Executive Hotel/Aberavon	144
Farmhouse Hotel/Llandogo	186
Ferry Restaurant/St Dogmael's	98
Fishguard Bay Hotel/Fishguard	100
Four Lanterns Restaurant/Barry	152
Gibson's Restaurant/Cardiff	162
Glansevin/Llangadog	132
Glantraeth/Bodorgan	62
Glendale Hotel/Penarth	158
Glyn-y-Mel/Fishguard	102
Golden Grove Inn/Rosset	37
Hand Hotel/Llangollen	27
Harvesters/Cardiff	160
Heatherslade Bay Hotel/Swansea	138
Henllys Hall Hotel/Beaumaris	58
Hotel 70 Degrees/Colwyn Bay	44
Ivy Bush Hotel/Carmarthen	128
Lake Vyrnwy Hotel/Llanwddyn	26
Lamb Hotel/Llangeler	93
Lanterns Restaurant/Cardiff	176
Linksway Hotel/Morfa Nefyn	66
Liver Inn/Rhydtalog	38
Lobster Pot/Rhydwyn	61
Locanda Restaurant/Cardiff	166
Malin House/Saundersfoot	124
Metropole Hotel/Llandrindod Wells	22
Moelwyn Restaurant/Criccieth	76
Osborne Hotel/Swansea	140
Owain Glyndwr Hotel/Corwen	28
Patron Restaurant/Beaumaris	56
Plas Maenan/Llanrwst	50
Plough Inn/Llandegla	34
Plymouth Arms/St Fagans	159
Porth Tocyn Hotel/Abersoch	68
Portmeirion/Penrhyndeudraeth	80
Positano Restaurant/Cardiff	167
Post House/Cardiff	177

Quaintways/Llantwit Major 146

Red Lion Hotel/Dinas Mawddwy 88
Robeston House/Robeston Wathen 126
Roman Embassy Restaurant/Cardiff 172
Royal Gate House Hotel/Tenby 122
Royal Goat Hotel/Beddgelert 77
Royal Hotel/Cardiff 170
Royal Oak Hotel/Welshpool 25
Royal Victoria Hotel/Llanberis 64
Ruthin Castle/Ruthin 32

Salutation Inn/Velindre 99
Saracen's Head/Beddgelert 78
Savastano's Restaurant/Cardiff 165
Seabank Hotel/Porthcawl 145
Six Bells Inn/Peterstone Wentlooge 178
Spot Restaurant/Cardiff 168
St Non's Hotel/St David's 112
Stables Restaurant/Llanwnda 65

Stradey Park Hotel/Llanelli 137
Sully House Restaurant/Swanbridge 154
Sygun Fawr Hotel/Beddgelert 79

Three Blackbirds/Llantarnam 183
Three Cocks Hotel/Brecon 21
Trefeddian Hotel/Aberdovey 89

Villa Pandana/Garndolbenmaen 75

Walnut Tree Inn/Llandewi Skirrid 19
Warpool Court Hotel/St David's 110
Waterloo Hotel/Betws-y-coed 52
Westgate Hotel/Newport 182
Whitesands Bay Hotel/St David's 104
Wrexham Crest Hotel/Wrexham 36

Ynyshir Hall/Eglwysfach 90
Ystafell Gymraeg/Cardiff 174

General index

afelia   152
aljotta   67
almond and lemon stuffing   94
almond cake   139
almonds   126, 146, 168
anchovy   30,48,61,83,146,156
Anglesey eggs   50
apple and damson mousse   70
apple and raspberry tart   23
apple baked   39
apple pudding   133
apples   31,68,70,108,120
apple tart Welsh   159
apricots   110,126
artichokes   71,100,116
artichoke soup   162
asparagus   116,144,173
asparagus and ham soufflé   113
aubergines fourées   80
Austrian coffee cake   95
avocado Edeyrnion   29
avocado soup cold   171
avocado with sea food   178

bacon   88,103,112,114,155,165,170
bain-marie   14
baked ham and parsley sauce   59
bamboo shoots   104
banana baked   147
bananas   77,93,130
banana trifle   74
bara brith   55
batter   135
beans green Chinese style   103
beans red kidney   121
béchamel sauce   14,50,80,82,93,113
beef
    boeuf à la Bourgignone   34
    boeuf des Marinieres   83
    casserole   34,83,108,121
    casseroled in cider   108
    chilli con carne   121

fillet   17,71,166,
    medallions   71
    Satay Indonesian   42
    steak and kidney   38
    strogonoff   179
    topside steak   34
    ox-tail   149
    Wellington   17
beer   58
beetroot   68
beignets soufflé   45
beurre-manié   39,91,114,154
beurre noisette   123
biscuits   138
blackbutter   47
Black Forest gâteau   106
boeuf à la Bourgignonne   34
boeuf des Marinieres   83
bouquet garni   14
braised lettuce with cucumber sauce   101
braised ox-tail   149
braised Welsh calves livers   131
brandy snaps/tulips   164
bread and butter pudding with pears   134
bread herb   132
bream   67
brisket   88
brith bara   55
brochette   86
broth
    game   28
    leek and potato mutton   128
Burgundy   52

cake   55,65,95,106,127,138,139
canneloni alla Vescovo   82
capers   47
captain's relish   68
Cardigan chicken   177
carré d'agneau en croûte   155
carrot and tomato soup   107
casserole of veal   92

cawl cennin Cymraeg   88
cennin-see leek
chasseur sauce   116
chateaubriand   116
cheese 50,58,85,90,175
cheese-cake with Kirsch   111
cheese sauce   176
cherries   31,64,106,109,130,165
chestnuts   49,140
chicken
    Cardigan   177
    casserole   25,39,52,78,110
    coq au vin   52
    escalopes sauté oriental   104
    estragon   37
    Gujarat   110
    in cider   39
    liver pâté   186
    Marengo   25
    Maryland   93
    petti di pollo alla Doney   183
    pie Maggie Gibson's   163
    pollo al ajillo   18
    poussin with peach   16
    Royale   78
    Snowdonia   174
    suprême Opera   44
    suprême Porthcawl   145
    velouté sauce   143
    Welsh   143
chilled apple and raspberry tart   23
chilli con carne   121
Chinese green beans   103
chipolata sausages   53
chocolate   49,75,89,106,161
chocolate crumb cake   138
chowder haddock   84
cider beef casseroled in   108
cinnamon   63
claret   73
cockles   50,82
cocoa   106,138
coconut   42,147
coffee cake   95

cold avocado soup   171
cold cucumber sauce   94
compote plum   139
coriander seeds   152
court-bouillon   142
coq au vin   52
crab dressed   79
crabmeat   177
cream and mustard sauce   23
crêpes aux fruits de mer   154
croquette potatoes   116
crown of Welsh lamb   22
cucumber   132
cucumber sauce   94,97,101
curry powder   24,42,102,130,136,168,
    171
custard   41,75
cutlets of veal Prince of Wales   175
Cyprus style fried potatoes   152
cyw iâr Eryri   174

damson and apple mousse   70
Dee salmon Glyndwr   30
demi-glace sauce   13,131
demi-sel cheese   90
devilled tomato sauce   85
dolmades   153
double saucepan   157
Dover sole   122
dressed crab   79
dressing salad   24
duck
    à l'orange   171
    Merioneth   31
    Osborne   140
duxelle   137

egg and honey pudding   41
eggs
    Anglesey   50
    fried rice   104
    soup   158
    surprise   129
entrecôte Apollo   173

escalopes sauté oriental   104
Espagnole sauce   13
estragon chicken   37

fillet de bœuf sauté strogonoff   179
fillet mignons à la Beaufremont   166
fillet of beef Wellington   17
fillet of brill Prince of Wales   27
fillets of sole casimir   168
fillet steak Cleopatra   144
fillet steak Roman Embassy   172
fish   50,100,154
   brill   27
   haddock   19,160
   kedgeree   160
   kipper pâté   76
   prawns   18,29,50,82,100,136,178,184
   salmon   30,50,86,100
   sewin   94,97
   skate   47
   sole   122,168
   soup   67
   stock   13,18,27,84,142
   trout   26
   tuna   68
   turbot   142
   velouté   142
flambé à la maître d'hôtel   165
fraises Marquise   115
French loaf   132
French onion soup   96
fresh orange with rum flavoured syrup   66
fresh pineapple and peaches in rum   109
fresh strawberry and melon flan   119
fried cheese stuffed mushrooms   85
fourées aubergines   80

gambas al ajillo   18
game
   broth   28
   hare   161
   pâté   81
   partridge   81
   pheasant   81,114
   quail   20
   rabbit   73,120
   stock   13,20,28,73,114,161
   venison   91
gammon steaks   46,152
garlic sauce   98
gâteau Black Forest   106
gâteau orange   127
gâteau strawberry   65
Gelert's pineapple   77
gigot d'agneau à la maison   56
ginger   103,164
golden chicken estragon   37
golwythau cig llo Tywysog Cymru   175
Grand Marnier   89,165,171
grapefruit cocktail   102
green beans Chinese style   103
green pepper sauce   22
grilled Mawddach salmon en brochette   86
guinea fowl   21
Gujarat chicken   110

haddock   160
haddock chowder   84
haddock smokies   19
ham   71,80,156,167
ham and asparagus soufflé   113
ham with parsley sauce   59
hare jugged   161
herb bread   132
herring roes   144
hollandaise sauce   100,112
honey   41,42,59,63,140
horseradish   26,178
horseradish sauce   93

ice cream   125,180,182
ice cream soufflé Grand Marnier   89
Indonesian Satay   42
Italian trifle   75

Jamaican baked bananas   147
jugged hare   161

kedgeree   160
kidney and steak pie   38
kidney beans   121
kidneys   23,32,123
kidneys Turbigo   53
kipper pâté   76

lamb
   carré d'agneau en croûte   155
   casserole   56
   crown   22
   cutlets   22
   kidneys   23,32
   noisettes/saddle   123
   Satay Indonesian   42
   shank   56
   shoulder   32
   sweetbreads   141
lapin façon paysanne   120
leek and potato mutton broth   128
leeks   50,56,67,92,143
leek soup   88,128
lemon and almond stuffing   94
lemon butter sauce   86
lemon mousse   124
lemons   79
lemon sauce   69
lentil soup   54
les escalopes de veau Marlborough   137
les pêches farcies   57
lettuce   72,101
liver pâté   186
livers   141,181
livers braised   131
lobster   78
   bisque   177
   Salutation   99
   Winterthur   61

Maggie Gibson's chicken pie   163
mandarin oranges   127
Marengo chicken   25
marinated gammon steaks   46
marinated raisin sauce   131

marrow Provençale   148
Marsala wine   75,157
Maryland chicken   93
mayonnaise   72,136,178
médaillons de veau Gourmet   169
medallions of fillet of beef Campania   71
melon and strawberry flan   119
melon dessert   180
melon salad with hot herb bread   132
Menai Pride mussel pâté   62
meringue   41,49,65
Mexican pineapple   181
minced meat   153
monkfish   82
Mont Blanc   49
mousse damson and apple   70
mousse lemon   124
mullet   67
mushrooms fried cheese stuffed   85
mushrooms in garlic sauce   98
mussel pâté   62
mussels   50,82,184
mussel sauce   142
mutton   32,128

Nelson's casserole   184
Neopolitan sauce   172
noisette sauce   123
noisettes of lamb Dinbych   123
noodles   156,166
Normandie sauce   21
Norwegian prawns   136
Norwegian style beetroot   68

Old Farmhouse chicken liver pâté   186
onion soup French   96
Opera chicken suprême   44
orange chiffon pie   35
orange duck   171
orange gâteau   127
oranges   31,77,164
orange sauce with pancakes   135
oranges with rum flavoured syrup   66
Osso bucco   48

192

ox-tail braised   149
oyster   178

pancakes in orange sauce   135
pancakes sweetcorn   123
pancakes unsweetened   154
paprika schnitzel   170
parsley sauce   59
partridge   81
pasta-see canneloni, spaghetti, tagliatelle
pastry   17,23,35,38,41,91,119,155,159,
   163
pâté   17,145,185
   captain's relish   68
   chicken liver   186
   Conca d'Oro   181
   game   81
   kipper   76
   mussel   62
   terrine de Sibier   81
   trout smoked   26
   tuna   68
peach   16,57,63,109,164,165
peach Snowdonia range   63
peanuts   42
pear and walnut salad   72
pears with bread and butter pudding   134
peppers stuffed   150
petti di pollo alla Doney   183
pheasant pâté   81
pheasant poivrade   114
pie chicken   163
pie orange chiffon   35
pie steak and kidney   38
pineapple   31,46,77,111,130,136,137,
   168
pineapple and peaches in rum   109
pineapple Mexican   182
plum compote with rich almond cake   139
pork
   chop Villa Borgese   36
   cutlets   152
   fillet   87,104,166
   minced   150

spare ribs   63
St Tudno sauce   50
tenderloin with prunes   146
with apricots and almonds   126
with lemon sauce   69
potato mutton and leek broth   128
potatoes   60,88,92,129
   croquette   116
   fried Cyprus style   152
   tŷ   159
poultry-see chicken, duck,guinea fowl
poussin stuffed with peach   16
prawn alagratin   176
prawns   18,29,50,82,100,122,136,178,
   184
Provençale marrow   148
Provençale sauce   124
Provençale scampi   124
prunes   146
puddings
   apple   133
   bread and butter with pears   134
   egg and honey   41
   Snowdon   64
purée   159

quails impatachio   20

rabbit
   peasants style   120
   stew with claret   73
raisins   64
raisin sauce   131
rarebit Welsh   58
reduction   14
rice   23,32,64,78,80,86,110,124,136,
   150,153,160,168,169,179
rice egg fried   105
rich almond cake   139
ris d'agneau Prince de Galles   141
risotto casimir   130
roast duck Osborne   140
roast guinea fowl-Normandie   21
roast loin of veal   69

roast shoulder of Welsh mutton 32
rösti 60
roux 142,143,154
Royale chicken 78
rum 49,66,95,109,147,157

saddle of lamb 123,155
saffron rice 86
sage leaves 167
Saint Tudno sauce 50
salad dressing 24,29
salad melon 132
salmon 50
  Dee Glyndwr 30
  grilled Mawddach 86
  steak Lady Jane 110
salpicon 178
saltimbocca alla Romana 167
Salutation lobster 99
Satay Indonesian 42
sauces
  aljotta 67
  Apollo 173
  Beaufremont 166
  béchamel 14,50,80,82,93,113
  Calvados 137
  caper 47
  chasseur 116
  cheese 176
  coconut 42
  cream and mustard 23
  cucumber 94,97,101
  demi-glace 13,131
  devilled tomato 85
  Espagnole 13
  fish 154
  for lobster 61
  garlic 98
  green pepper 22
  hollandaise 112
  horseradish 93
  leek 67
  lemon 69
  lemon butter 86

  marinated raisin 131
  mussel 142
  mustard 144
  Neopolitan 172
  noisette 123
  Normandie 21
  orange 135
  paprika 170
  parsley 59
  prawn 122
  Prince of Wales 175
  Provençale 124
  Saint Tudno 50
  smitaine 87
  Snowdonia 174
  tomato 151
  velouté 142,163,177
  Villa Borgese 36
  white 50,76
sausage meat 150
sausage 53
sauté 14
sautéed lamb kidneys 23
sauté of chicken in cider 39
scallops 184
scallops à la creme 118
scallops maison 112
scampi 178,184
scampi Provençale 124
schwarzwalder kirschtorte 106
seafood with avocado 178
seafood with pancakes 154
sewin 95,97
shrimps 61,82,102
Sibier terrine de 81
skate 47
smoked haddock chowder 84
smoked trout pâté 26
Snowdonia chicken 174
Snowdon pudding 64
sole casimir 168
sole fourée 122
soufflé ham and asparagus 113
soufflé ice cream 89

soup
  Aljotta   67
  artichoke   162
  avocado cold   171
  carrot and tomato   107
  cawl cennin   88
  fish   67,84
  game   28
  haddock   84
  leek   88
  leek and potato mutton   128
  lentil   54
  onion French   96
  smoked haddock chowder   84
  stracciatella   158
paghetti   87,166
paghetti alla carbonara   165
pare ribs in honey and cinnamon   63
ponge   65,127
tables strawberry gâteau   65
teak
  Apollo   173
  chateaubriand   116
  Cleopatra   144
  escalopes sauté oriental   104
  in wine   54
  medallions Campania   71
  Roman Embassy   172
  tournedos Beaufort   185
teak and kidney pie   38
ew rabbit   73
ock   13
racciatella soup   158
rawberries   115
rawberry and melon flan   119
rawberry gâteau   65
rogonoff beef   179
uffed mushrooms   85
uffed peppers   150
uffing   21,32
uffing lemon and almond   94
uprême of chicken Portcawl   145
uprême of chicken Opera   44
urprise eggs   129

suryn San Tudno   50
sweet corn   93,116,123
sweet paste   41
sweets
  apple pudding   138
  Austrian coffee cake   95
  banana trifle   74
  beignets soufflé   45
  Black Forest gâteau   106
  brandy tulips   164
  bread and butter pudding with pears 134
  cheese cake with Kirsch   111
  chilled apple and raspberry tart   23
  chocolate crumb cake   138
  coffee cake   95
  damson and apple mousse   70
  egg and honey pudding   41
  flambé à la maître d'hôtel   165
  fraises Marquis   115
  Gelert's pineapple   77
  ice cream soufflé Grand Marnier   89
  Italian trifle   75
  Jamaican baked bananas   147
  lemon mousse   125
  les pêches farcies   57
  Mont Blanc   49
  mousse   70,125
  orange chiffon pie   35
  orange gâteau   127
  orange with rum flavoured syrup   66
  pancakes in orange sauce   135
  peaches stuffed   57
  peach Snowdonia range   63
  pineapple and peaches in rum   109
  pineapple Gelert's   77
  plum compote with rich almond cake 139
  Snowdon pudding   64
  soufflé   89
  Stables strawberry gâteau   65
  strawberries and Kirsch   115
  syllabub   79
  trifle   74,75
  Welsh apple tart   159
  zabaglione   157

zuppa Inglese   75
syllabub   79
syrup   138,164

tagliatelle Alfredo   156
tarragon   37
tart Welsh apple   159
tea   55,146
tenderloin pork   146
terrine de Sibier   81
tomato and carrot soup   107
tomatoes   132,148,156
tomato Gervais   90
tomato sauce   151
tournedos Beaufort   185
traditional Welsh cawl   88
trifle banana   74
trifle Italian   75
trout smoked pâté   26
tuna fish   68
Turbigo kidneys   53
turbot with mussel sauce   142
tŷ potatoes   159

veal
    casserole   48,92
    cutlets   156,175
    escalopes   137,156,170
    loin   69

médaillons   169
Osso bucco   48
risotto casimir   130
saltimbocca alla Romana   167
stock   17
vittello Pizziaola   156
    with lemon sauce   69
velouté sauce   142,163,177
venison in pastry   91
vermicelli   89
Vescovo canneloni   82
vine leaves   153

walnuts   72
watercress   46
weights and measures   15
Welsh apple tart   159
Welsh chicken   143
Welsh rarebit   58
white sauce   50,76
whole grilled Teifi sewin   94
wine steak in   54
wings of skate with capers   47
Winterthur lobster   61
wyau Môn   50

zabaglione Caprice   157
zest   171
zuppa Inglese   75